THE SECRETS OF BUILDING A

SUCCESSFUL

HIGH TICKET BUSINESS SALES CLOSER

DAVID WAUGH

stanfordpub.com

<u>Let me promise you this upfront</u>: By the end of the book you'll fully understand step-by-step exactly how I reached a situation within just a few months of starting my online coaching business of earning over $10,000 / month while traveling and working 10 - 15 hours per week!

This book will show you everything you need to know about starting your own online business and making a great profit early on. None of the stuff I'm going to teach you is going to take 6 months or years. The 2 main reasons most people never start is because:

1. They don't believe they can do it.
2. They think it'll take too long to do it.

First I'm going to help you understand WHY you can do it yourself, second I'm going to help you understand HOW you can do it in just a few weeks. Everything I teach is designed for speed and practical action. My goal for you is that you'll start making at-least $1,000 within the first 2 weeks or so because I know that when I got started I wanted to see results early or I would get discouraged.

Let me emphasize that this is not about being a pushy salesman, spamming people or scamming them, this book will give you a quick overview of the steps I took to launch multiple consulting businesses and selling products, every time I launch a business I know it'll make at-least $2,000 on its first month, <u>even if this is a new industry where no-one knows me.</u> This is because I work with a few simple game-changing understandings that I will share with you here that allow me to shortcut all the tough work usually associated with making money online (or in any business venture for that matter..).

I did it all with my 5-Step Blueprint:

1. **Sell High-Ticket Items:** I'll show you how to sell services and products worth over $1,000 starting right now, starting from discovering what high-ticket items you can start selling immediately and why it's actually easier to sell high-ticket items than cheap shit.

2. **Find Your Ideal Clients:** You can't properly sell high-ticket items if you don't also match them with the right person who's interested and willing to buy them. I'll show you how to identify exactly who your perfect client is and how to get them to approach you.

3. **The Killer Business Model:** Once you have a high-ticket product and you know who your ideal clients are, it's all about know how get them to approach you. I'll show you the 3-step blueprint the most successful entrepreneurs use to create customers. This will dramatically simplify, improve and demystify for you the process of making sales in any market and with any product.

4. **Business Automation:** It's not enough to have a business that makes great money, it's also important to integrate it into your new lifestyle by automating the process of getting customers, either by hiring people (I'll show you how), by investing money in marketing (I'll show you how), or by making the marketing part of your awesome life (I'll show you how).

5. **Common Pitfalls & Mistakes (Bonus!):** I'll help you avoid the mistakes that will make you fail, after that I'll help you avoid the mistakes that will make you fail AFTER you succeeded, which is much, much more painful. Trust me - don't miss this chapter.

Who is this book for?

This book is perfect for any entrepreneur who's starting out and wanting to make the most amount of money in the least amount of time without doing something annoying, spammy, scammy or otherwise. This book will keep you from being overwhelmed, you'll know exactly what to focus on and have a perfect roadmap to getting to big online income.

If you're already an entrepreneur you should check this book out as a refresher to remember the fundamentals of running a successful online business and having a great time doing it. It's easy to get caught up in the minutia instead of what actually matters, as one of my mentors likes to say *"If you focus on minutia, you get MANURE!"*. Couldn't agree with him more!

This book is also meant for employees who are looking to quit their 9-to-5 job and become more independant (and maybe even travel!). You don't have to quit your job yet and can quickly replace your salary in a month or two if you put in a couple of hours to make this happen!
If you find yourself in one of those categories, or even in a hybrid of them, it means you're going to have a very good time reading this and learning about everything.

read this! If by the end of this book you're not filled with passion, enthusiasm and a clear knowing of what to do next, just let me know and I'll be happy to help.

Step 1. Sell High-Ticket Items

I'll begin this first chapter by being brutally honest here. You probably haven't made a single dollar online yet (or maybe some pocket change at best). You picked up this guide out of some dim light of inspiration and hope, thinking "Maybe this will finally be the time I find that missing nugget of information that will show me the roadmap, the path to making my dream of making money online come true."

This book will definitely give you that and much more.

Let's get this one nugget out of the way first, the single biggest secret that I've learned which has allowed me to easily make tens of thousands of dollars online in just months of opening any online business is this:

Selling high-ticket products is fucking easy.

When I wanted to start my first online business the only thing I cared about was seeing money come into my PayPal account and as much of it as possible, no matter how; and I'm sure that if I'd ask you you'd say that you would love to start by making these big $1,000, $2,000, $3,000 sales and more, seeing thousands of dollars go into your bank account <u>every single day.</u>

Unfortunately through, through bad conditioning you've been led to have many bad beliefs and excuses about charging "big-bucks", so you archive that idea in the back of your head and compromise, "what the next best thing?", and you start thinking of ways of selling something cheap! (Classic low-self-esteem, you probably do this in other areas of your life too)

No harm there right? (**<u>Seriously</u>, think back how many times you've made this instinctive compromise when creating a plan**)

Sure, you can start with nice low-ticket items, nice, harmless, low-risk, sounds **easy** right? Soon you'll be selling them like cupcakes!

So you start by creating a low-ticket product, of-course, because it's cheap you don't really put that much effort into it (compare this for example to the book you're reading now, 40+ pages of FREE GOLD), that you've created your cheap product as an excuse for someone to pay you a little bit of money, it's time to try to sell it!

This brings you to the first problem, a basic math problem, and the problem is that the "real" money doesn't come from low-ticket products (unless your goal is <u>barely scratching</u> a $1,000 / month for the first few months <u>at-best</u>).

Marketers don't usually make money from low-ticket products, they just use them as a gateway filter for the people who will actually pay for the expensive stuff (high-ticket products). Low-ticket items are also used as a way to pay for ad traffic that later turns into high-ticket sales through the funnel (with maybe a bit of profit left after marketing costs).

No biggie right? You can still make a bit of money from selling low-ticket items. But what if you're aiming to make $5,000 / month? This brings us to the second and bigger problem; let me break down for you what happens on the level of conversions when you try to make your dreams come true by selling cheap products:

Let's say that you start with a low-ticket product, you'll probably use a squeeze page, this means you'll also need to create a free gift to entice people into your mailing list, let's say 40% of your visitors convert and leave their email addresses, you then immediately redirect them to a sales page for your low-ticket product (just like I did to you with my $47 product). Then, on average, about 5% of those people that got to the sales page would actually buy the low-ticket item (**assuming** you have solid marketing, web design, pitch, copywriting, offer, etc..).

This means you need about 50 unique visitors to get 1 sales of $7 to $47. If your goal is to make an extra $5,000 / month online you'll need anywhere between 106 to 714 sales (excluding taxes, marketing costs, refunds, services costs and PayPal fees) just to reach your goal, which if you've been following means you'll need about 5,300 to 35,500 website visitors either through organic traffic or paid for with ads.

Let's look at a different situation from the same framework:

Let's say you start with a high-ticket product or service, you can either create a 15-hour course for anywhere between $997 to $2997 or simply offer your services (we'll discuss this later) for $997 / month etc.

Instead of going through the whole mailing list and low-ticket item process (which is used to supplement the high-ticket item, make clients more willing to spend big money, and to cover the marketing costs etc..) the only thing you're going to want to do is get as many people "on the phone" as possible (to be more specific - them applying for some sort of free consultation or demonstration either face-to-face, on Skype video or just on audio).

When you're trying to close people for high-ticket products you're going to want to start with this sort of conversion funnel:

Super Converting High-Ticket Funnel:
Person Watches Your Content -> Person Visits Your Website, Sees Free Consultation Offer -> Person Applies For Said Free Consultation -> You Close the Person on the Phone.

Let's break this down in-terms of numbers, **earlier we talked about roughly 2.5% of your visitors buying a $7 to $47 product.**

In the case of the "**Super Converting High-Ticket**", we get the following numbers: about 5% of the people will apply for a free coaching call, about 80% would show up, about 15% would buy the high-ticket product/service.

I'm not really a math-wiz but with a calculator you can safely see that you need almost 25 visitors to get a free consultation call, and you need about 6 free consultation calls to close a $1,000+ sale.

In-terms of visitors this means you need about 150 visitors to close a $1,000, or a total of 750 monthly visitors to reach your goal of $5,000, the best part is that you can usually get that much traffic organically just by posting videos and articles on YouTube, forums etc.. and the cherry on the pie is that you can pay for ads to get that traffic and easily cover the costs (each coaching call is "worth" $150+ since you only need about 6 to close a sale), if each ad click (website visit) costs you $1, and you need about 150 visits to get 6 consultation calls to close a $1,000 sale, this means you can invest $150 in marketing to get a sale of $1,000.

Sorry for all the math.

I've been postponing your excuses for some time now, so let's get them all handled:

But Robby! **"Shouldn't I start by selling cheap products first?"**

But Robby! **"How do I sell expensive shit if I never even sold cheap shit?"**

But Robby! **"Why would someone pay me and not someone better?"**

But Robby! **"Shouldn't I get some credentials before I go for it?"**

First of all, I don't believe for one second that somebody who's reading this book would actually have nothing to offer. Almost everyone who is attracted to my materials has at least one thing that they're really really good at , And does Alan Watts said, "when you're really good at something, there's always someone is willing to pay for it".if you honestly don't have anything that you're good at, you need to learn a skill. If you really have no skills at all, either you're seriously underestimating yourself or you should close this book and spend half a year oh so getting really good at something.

Did you know that selling expensive things is actually easier than selling cheap things?

Let me tell you a story about a client of mine named Ivan, Ivan was a fitness teacher who is an absolute master of fitness and diet. The guy built an amazing course and also offered private coaching. He would post content on YouTube and Facebook and also answer peoples questions at forms in groups.

Ivan would get about five people for a free consultation every week. He would try to sell them his course or his coaching for about $100 or so. On his best days Ivan would close about 10% of his free coaching calls which he spent over an hour each on.

The first bad news was that the people Ivan would close almost always wound end up being shit clients (meaning, not achieving any results or just flat out quit midway).

The second bad news was that the 90% of his calls that wouldn't purchase consistently gave him the absolute worst attitude and excuses. Ivan would hear on a daily basis questions like:

"Can you give me the first week for free?"

"Why do you think you're worth my money?"

"Why are you charging $100? Why not less?"

"Can you coach me for free and I'll pay you if it works?"

Yup. With a daily barrage of condescending people while making almost no money, Ivan felt almost completely discouraged and disrespected.

At this point I started working with Ivan, he described me his situation in order for me to troubleshoot the source of his predicament. Ivan was clearly expecting some complex, behind-the-scenes, incredible guru answer involving many microscopic changes that would add-up into an amazing result after a few months; Instead all he heard from me was "**raise your prices from $100 to $1,000 and your problem will be immediately solved**".

As expected, Ivan was very reluctant and hesitant to do the big jump, he had exactly the same excuses I've listed above. The conversation would usually look like this:

Robby: *"Raise your prices to $1,000".*

Ivan: *"But I don't know if I'm worth it yet."*

Robby: *"How good do you think your knowledge and skills are?"*

Ivan: *"The best. I know everything there is to know."*

Robby: *"So raise your prices to $1,000".*

Ivan: *"But what if they say NO?"*

Robby: *"They're already saying NO".*

And this is how it went what seemed like forever. We almost always resist the things that will help us the most. This back-and-forth went on for almost 3 more weeks. 3 weeks of shit calls and no money finally built up the frustration needed for him to say "FUCK IT" and give it a chance. He truly had nothing more to lose.

From this point on all Ivan changed was this - When the time came to state the price of his coaching or course, Ivan would say $1,000 instead of the usual $100.

Instantly, the magic happened.

Ivan started closing every 5rd or 6th call for roughly $1,000 per sale. This was incredible for him since Ivan comes from Eastern Europe where the average domestic monthly salary is about $500.

The change was instantaneous and amazing, people started treating him with respect and admiration, his demeanour changed and his self-esteem shot through the roof, almost everyone wanted his coaching or course (not everyone could pay), he would literally tell me stories about people begging him to let them pay half upfront and the rest later etc..

This might sound like an amazing turn of events but anyone who sold high-ticket items knows it's just the way it works. When you know what you're doing (or can scam people into thinking you know what you're doing) and you know how to ask for the right price, people react to you in a very different way, you become a leader.

There are many psychological reasons why selling high-ticket items ($1,000+) so easy in a <u>phone, video or face-to-face sales</u> (I'll explain in the 3rd chapter how to do these calls in a 100% super fun, easy, lighthearted and effortless way with a 15% to 20% closing ratio).

To quote a previous mentor of mine, "The few calls you make will be scary, awkward and probably suck. Once you get used to it, these calls will become the best and most fun part of your day, you're actually going to look forward to them!"

When I just got started with offering consultation calls I froze, talked weird and all that stuff, once I got used to them they really became the best part of my day. To this day I can't think of anything more fun than having a great

2-3 hour coaching call; and that's really what it is for me, just a free coaching call, where I happen to say "if you want more, the price is X for 2 months upfront". We'll go much more in-depth in Chapter 3.

Anyway, the reason selling high-ticket items is a lot easier than regular items is because of what I like to call "Tangible VS. Intangible selling". I'll explain the concept in the most simplistic way possible:

When you go buy a wallet, there are the regular "mass-market" wallets ($10-$30), and then there's the "prestigious" Louis Vuitton wallets ($100-$300).

Have you ever wondered WHY they can charge 10x more for a product that basically does the same thing? Simple - they label themselves as a prestigious brand.

When someone is selling you a cheap wallet, you enter a "market" mentality, you start comparing prices, you ask very logical questions about the product and so on..

On the other hand, when someone is selling you something that you feel is "prestigious", you tend to enter a more emotional mode because now your self-esteem is involved, so you focus much less on the "technical" details of the sale and a lot more about the "feelings" you get before buying it.

The good news is that you don't have to convince an entire nation that your brand is the prestigious type that costs a lot, all you really need to do is give great value to the person you're talking too in the form of knowledge, guidance etc.. and when the time comes to close the deal you simply say "the product costs $1497, do you prefer 1 or 2 payments?", and just by talking about the price in a nonchalant way (this has to be genuine though) you automatically label yourself as a prestigious brand, because what goes on in the customer's head is "Wow, if he's saying this price to me and he's so relaxed about it that must mean a lot of people buy from him, this means I want this product too!".

Seriously, it's that simple.

As a small side-note though - you will get that true confidence and nonchalant attitude about the price once 1 or 2 people actually pay you $1,000+ for your product or service and you see that they are actually happy about it. Until then you just kind of "fake it" and cross your fingers the first 2-3 calls!

Another small sidenote, the more people pay you, the more they tend to value and use whatever product or service you gave them, so the more money you can get them to pay you, the more value they'll get and the better reviews you'll get later. The opposite is also true.

Funny how this works ha?

Anyway, I hope this covers the idea of high-ticket products and why the fastest, easiest way to reach your first big online business milestone (making $5,000 / month) is to **start by selling the expensive shit first - and "worry" about the cheap shit later.**

Step 1. Summary:

- Selling high-ticket products is EASY (if you follow a few simple steps).
- Starting out by selling cheap products is ALWAYS* the wrong decision.
  * Unless the cheap products are used as a supplement to your high-ticket products by covering the marketing expenses and making clients more receptive to buying more expensive products.
- You can easily make a "detour" and go straight to selling $1,000 products if you follow the business model detailed in Step 3.
- It takes over 25,000 monthly visitors to close 135 sales of a $37 product for a total of $5,000 / month with almost no expenses.
- It takes just 750 monthly visitors to close 5 sales of a $1,000 product for a total of $5,000 / month with a lot of marketing expenses.
- Almost everyone has something they're really good at that they can sell for over $1,000 to someone who's really into that thing.
- The higher the price of something the more prestigious it seems. It's actually easier to sell a $5,000 handbag than it is to sell a $50 one.
- The more people pay you the more they value and use your products, that's why you're never going to hear someone complain about a Mercedes or a Louis Vuitton handbag (besides how much they paid).
- Your ticket to success and freedom is being able to sell just 3-4 high-ticket items <u>per month</u>, which is extremely easy when you know follow all the steps in this guide.

Step 2. Find Your Ideal Clients

A business blueprint would not be complete without a specific guide to targeting and finding your ideal customers. The only way to reach optimal conversion rates is by targeting ideal customers.

If you want to sell high-ticket products you need to find someone who 1. Has the financial ability to buy and 2. Is more than willing to spend good money for it.

Let's say you are in the fitness business and are aiming to sell a high-ticket products, in this situation we can break down several qualities of every person you will interact through your marketing and sales process:

1. Interest In Topic.
2. Financial Situation.
3. Affinity Factor.

When you find someone that is both interested in the topic, has a good financial situation and has great chemistry with you, selling is automatic, effortless and fun. I don't even talk to anyone who I'm not sure is at-least a 7 out of 10 in all 3 areas, I love my high-ticket sales to be the most fun and easy part of my day.

Interest In Topic: The first and most important thing is, just how interested is this person in the topic of your business? You can easily get a sense of where a person is in-terms of interest from a scale of 1 to 10, with 1 being "I couldn't care less about this" to 10 being "I will give up anything to improve at this".

Depending on what you're aiming for in your business (are you aiming to make as much money as possible as fast as possible, or are you aiming to steadily build and strong and wide audience) you might decide to put a cap on the lowest level of interest you'll deal with.

For example, some people have a funnel of products with increasing prices, a ladder from $7, to $37, to $237, to $2,370 and even $23,700. This way they can target the lowest interest groups and slowly increase their interest.

In the opposite way you can basically go straight for the hot potatoes, the 8s, 9s and 10s in-terms of interest in fitness who are already looking to go all the way with someone. For the purpose of this guide and selling high-ticket products (again, this is about making as much money as fast as possible, so we're going straight to the highest prices first, the people that will give you $2,000+ dollars after a 2-3 hours conversation. Not slowly building an audience).

So in this case (trying to close only a $1,000+ product / service) we are going to focus on the 8, 9 and 10 clients in-terms of interest. We'll talk in Step 3 about the process of filtering leads (potential clients) based on interest level to only spend time on the most likely to close for $1,000+ in a matter of HOURS.

Financial Situation: This one is pretty self-explanatory but bears highlighting. I've spent countless hours trying to close with people who just didn't have the money. It took me months of painful experiences to finally decide to start filtering people to some extent based on finances.

The truth is, some people just don't have the money, or are so financially tight that you'd rather they won't pay you because they'll become needy and dependant on you (I'll explain in a moment).

We can classify people into 3 financial groups:

1. Can easily afford your product.
2. Can barely afford your product.
3. Can't afford your product.

You want 80% of your clients to be in the 1st group and only 20% of them to be in the 2nd group.

The reason you want to be careful with people that can barely afford your product is that they are a mixed bag, some are really cool people that just happen to not have a lot of money (some of my best clients were people like these, I was also a person like that when I was starting out).

On the other hand, most of the people that can barely afford your product are people who are really bad at life to be honest and will end up putting all their hopes on your product or service "changing their life", these people will take up a ton of your time, won't produce any result, and most will even complain later or ask for a refund or fade into obscurity because they "failed again" at everything.

It's really unhealthy to deal with people like this so I highly recommend staying away from anyone who can just barely afford your product if he or she have even a bit of the stench of a negative vibe (judgmental thinking, really stupid questions, etc'.) or negative life story ("I'm just a loser", "nothing I try works", etc'.)

Regarding people who can't afford your product to begin with, it's important to filter them out from the start so that you don't spend any time talking to them (unless you don't mind giving a bit of your time pro-bono).

I'll talk more about building your business model to automatically filter out the 2nd and 3rd group in the Step 3.

Affinity Factor: This is only important if you actually want to coach people instead of selling a product where you don't have to actually be present to deliver value.

I personally focused for a few years on coaching people 1-on-1 through Skype, I'd coach about 1 client per day so about 2 hours of work per day. Each client would pay me up to $3,000 for 2-3 hours of my time per week for 2 months (about $150 per hour of "work").

Let me tell you this: when you coach positive people that you have great chemistry with, time flies. Some of my best ideas came from good coaching session, I can definitely rank coaching among the top 3 things I enjoy most in my life.

Another thing you should know is this: coaching people you don't have great chemistry with is at best boring and at worst absolutely horrible. Trust me on this - don't close ANYONE whom you're not sure yet.

Working with the right client, someone with whom I have great chemistry with and also a strong intuition that I can help them is my absolute top priority. These days when I do accept coaching clients I don't even try to close them, all I do is filter out people until I find my ideal client, that person is the easiest close you've ever had, at any price.

Sometimes I might talk a full 2 hours with someone and get to know them and their goals, if at any point they really seem like they might be ideal clients I'll simply ask them "my coaching at this time is $5,000 for 2 months, if you are interested in working with me I'd like to have a 2nd free call with you just to make sure you're a perfect fit". (<u>I have 100% closing rate with this line</u>, no joke.)

Step 2. Summary:

- Write down a description of your ideal client based on the 3 characteristics of a potential client (Interest in Topic, Financial Situation, Affinity Factor).
- The higher your price the more interested the people you target need to be in your topic of business.
- Make sure 80% of your focus is on people who can afford your products with some exception to people who can barely afford your products. Make sure to completely filter out people who can't afford your products.
- If you are selling a product or service that require you to interact with the client often, make sure you only close the people that you have a very high affinity with.
- When you find people that represent the holy trinity (Extremely interested in your topic, can easily buy your product, have great chemistry with you) they end up paying you <u>automatically</u> and <u>without effort</u>.

Step 3. The Killer Business Model

Welcome to Step 3!

Glad you got this far.

Excited? You should be. Here's where everything we've learned about sales and traffic turns into a simple, easy to follow business model that can start pulling you thousands of dollars with easy high-ticket sales.

Let me remind you:

Your ticket to success and freedom is being able to sell just 3-4 high-ticket items <u>per month</u>, which is extremely easy when you know follow all the steps in this guide.

If you take the business model that I'll teach you here and apply it consistently for a few weeks, you're practically guaranteed to make 1 or 2 $1,000+ sales <u>by the end of first month</u>.

Before we get into the business model, let's discuss the term "Sales Funnels" which I used a bit in Step 1 and which we're going to discuss deeply in this step.

What are Sales Funnels?

Sales Funnels are basically the steps that a potential client takes from the moment you first interact all the way to the final sale.

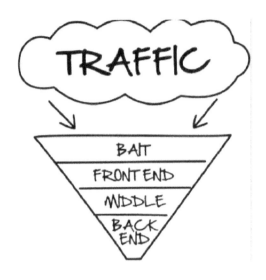

Sales Funnel figure by Russell Brunson

The example above is the most basic and common type of sales funnel, first you have Traffic (visitors) that are coming either organically (for free) through YouTube or a Blog, or through paid ads like those on Facebook or Google.

The Traffic comes because of a free Bait (like the free 5-Step Blueprint you're currently reading), the bait is easy to get and the only thing you have to "pay" for it is your email address, the purpose of the Bait is to give you enough value to "get you through the door" in-terms of being receptive to buying something cheap later and also getting your email for further marketing efforts.

The reason the bait is always used to get your email is to capture as much of the traffic as possible for use later. The more emails, subscribers, followers you have the more traffic you can control for free. ALWAYS get people's emails, even if you're not going to use them yet. Trust me on this, I have about 3,000+ emails I missed because I never knew how important they are and I regret every single one I don't have!

Once you take the Bait you progress to the Front End (like the 300+ pages Evolution of a Maniac book I've offered you ((Great opportunity to purchase for just $37 if you haven't done so already: https://goo.gl/VBjpqt))), the Front End is a higher from of value but it's also a higher form of investment.

Notice that the value is always proportional to the investment. You might get to know me and pay me $1,000 for just a couple hours of my time - but I doubt you'll want to do that if we just met and I told you "Hey do you want to pay me $1,000 for a couple hours of talking?". You need to gradually build up the value and then gradually increase the price.

Anyway the next 2 steps (the Middle and Back End) simply refer to even higher levels of value and also higher levels of prices. Once you've bought a $37 product and got more value than you've paid for, you'll probably consider paying $370 for the next product, and once you've got more value than you've paid for again, you'll probably consider paying $3,700 for the next product, rinse - repeat.

Remember that not everyone will go up to the highest level of the sales funnel, 85% of the people are OK with just getting the free book, out of those that got the free book about 10% will buy the $37 product, out of those that bought the $37 product about 15% will also buy the $370 and so on.. That's why the more traffic you get the better the results.

Also keep in mind that this classic sales funnel has been used since man began selling things, and will continue to be used as long as people sell things. It's not some trend or strategy, just human psychology that can be applied in any area of life (anyone who tried to pick up a guy or a girl knows what I'm talking about (("Let's go upstairs for a quick drink" is the classic Front End bait to a Back End which funny enough even sounds like we're talking about sex))).

So just to summarise, the sales funnel is basically a series of incremental steps where every step offers more value at a higher price, most people stay at the low steps, some people jump straight to the high steps, <u>you focus on helping those are climbing all the steps</u>.

The whole point of a sales funnel is that the deeper you go the less people there will be, but if you get enough traffic into the funnel and you provide great value, at-least some percentage of people will reach the end (your most expensive product or service).

Here's an example of a few situations in an average funnel based on the amount of traffic:

Classic Sales Funnel	Example A	Example B	Example C
Monthly Traffic	1,000	5,000	25,000
Free Bait (50%)	500	2,500	12,500
$37 Front End (10%)	50	250	1,250
$297 Middle (10%)	5	25	125
$1497 Back End (10%)	0.5	2.5	12.5
Front End Income	$1,850	$9,250	$46,250

Middle Income	$1,485	$7,425	$37,125
Back End Income	$748	$3,742	$18,712
Total Income	$4,083	$20,417	$102,087

As you can see, you create a value ladder with increasing prices and value, the purpose of the funnel is to capture as much average dollar value per every visitor as possible.

Most of the time when people want to start their online business they'll go for the low-hanging fruit (the low-ticket items) and try to sell cheap stuff without actually building a full funnel for it. I've explained why this is wrong in detail in Step 1.

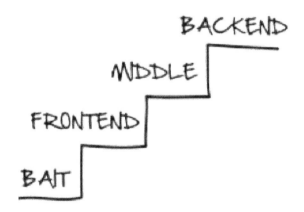

Value Ladder figure by Russell Brunson

So this is what a classic sales funnel looks like when displayed in a value-ladder format, as you can see you get value from Bait, then go up in price to Front End, then you get value from Front End, then go up in price to Middle...

Here's where I like to do things differently:

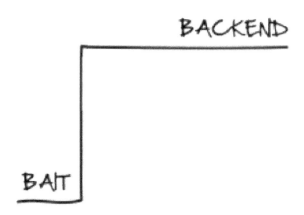

Who said you can't jump straight to the top?

Did you know that instead of slowly creating a value ladder, building each product at a time, spending months of learning and work to maximize your growth, you can just jump straight to selling the high-ticket item?

Notice I still offer a bait, this is <u>mandatory</u>, you can't just go up to people and ask them to pay you $1,000+ for your product or service, but instead of a free eBook, you can actually offer them a <u>free consultation call</u> and then all you need to do is to offer them enough value in a 2-3 hour call and the right people (about 15% if you filter them like I'll show you in a moment) will jump on the offer and go straight to your highest priced offer!

Don't misunderstand me for one moment and think that I'm telling you that from now on you're only going to close $1,000+ sales and you'll always have to do that and that's your business, on one hand in Step 4 I'm going to teach you how to <u>scale</u> the business and make it grow by automating stuff so you have other people getting you traffic, doing the calls and making the sales while you keep most of the profit. On the other hand I'm also going to show you how to build your funnel <u>while</u> getting the BIG MONEY straight from the beginning!

This is the type of funnel I want you to start with (Robby's Sales Funnel):

Robby's Sales Funnel	Example A	Example B	Example C
Traffic	1,000	5,000	25,000
Free Bait (50%)	500	2,500	12,500
Free Consultation (20%)	100	500	2500
Qualify For Call (33%)	33	167	833
$1497 Sale (20%)	6.6	33.4	166
Total Income	**$9,880**	**$50,149**	**$248,502**

As you can see, when you reduce the funnel down to the bare minimum your conversions get MUCH higher and it's a lot easier to reach the goal. Before we break down the funnel step-by-step, notice just how little traffic you need to get to reach the $5,000 per month goal.

For every 1,000 new visitors, we get about 500 people leaving their emails, then being redirected to a free consultation application from. About 100 people would apply for the free consultation. Out of those only 33 would qualify for the call (we have high standards). And finally, out of the 33 calls you should expect NO LESS than 20% closing ratio (I'll explain more about the sales call towards the end of the chapter), this means you make 6-7 sales and earn almost $10,000.

Anyone who is a successful internet marketer will tell you that these numbers and conversion rates are average, not too high and not too low. I definitely neglected to take into account small details like the fact that about 20% of the people who applied for the call just don't show up at all, but even if you cut the numbers I showed you in half, I believe it they would still be quite impressive and way beyond your current goals or what you thought was possible with so little effort.

If we break down the numbers even further you can see that 1,000 visitors would result in almost $10,000 with our funnel, this means that every visit is worth about $10 for you.

If you currently make a $2,000 salary by working 130 hours for $15, you can completely replace that income in weeks with just 2 sales of $1,000. To close 2 sales you need about 10 free consultation calls, which means you need about 350 monthly visits to your site. That's just over 10 visits per day.

Do you think you can get 10 people to click on a link to visit your site by offering them a free gift every day?

Just to state the obvious, we're talking about relevant people from Western society, I'm not talking about your Mom or a pirate from Somalia.

So..... Back to business,

Let's break down how to do EACH step in the funnel:

Traffic: People visit your website because of your Free Bait (a free eBook or something else that sounds really nice), it's extremely easy to do marketing for free stuff, how hard would it be for you to come up to a stranger in the street and offer them a something free that's worth a lot (just think how much this book is worth to you, and you got it for free. Shameless plug - Get My $37 Book!).

As mentioned before, there are basically 3 way to get traffic (technically 4), the first way is using Organic Traffic, the second is using Paid Traffic, the third is using Traffic You Own, and the fourth is Indirect Traffic.

Let's break down all 4:

- **Organic Traffic:** This is traffic that you "naturally" create using things like Facebook posts, YouTube videos, Google Search, Blog Posts etc. Basically assets that you create online that generate traffic. What I love about organic traffic is the fact that it keeps giving you passive traffic, I have videos I've made months ago that still give me views to this day. Personally I love organic traffic the most simply because I love creating content.

- **Paid Traffic:** This is traffic that you pay for, simple as that. We're talking about Facebook Ads, Google Ads, YouTube Ads, Paid Promotions, Banners etc. The good thing about this kind of traffic is that it's basically unlimited, the bad thing is that it costs money. The deeper your funnel the more you can afford to pay to create clients and whoever can outspend the competition wins. If you recall in Robby's Sales Funnel we estimated that every view is worth about $10. That means as long as you pay less than a whopping $10 per click/visitor you'll basically make a profit. Don't tell me we don't do magic here   (NOTICE: when I say "you'll make money as long as you spend less than $10 per click/visitor", I mean <u>after</u> you made a few sales and know exactly how much your traffic is worth, not before! Don't be stupid and spend all your saved up money on ads yet capiche?).

- **Traffic You Own:** This is traffic that you control in the literal sense of the word, things like your emails list, blog followers, YouTube subscribers etc. Basically traffic that you can directly advertise to whenever you like, however much you like, and basically for free.
- **Indirect Traffic:** This is traffic that comes from referrals, mentions etc. You don't have any control of this traffic, just make sure to redirect as much of it to Squeeze Pages (Free Bait) to capture as much of the traffic as possible and turn it into Traffic You Own so that you can actually control it later.

Here are 2 examples of banners that get traffic into your Free Bait / Squeeze Page:

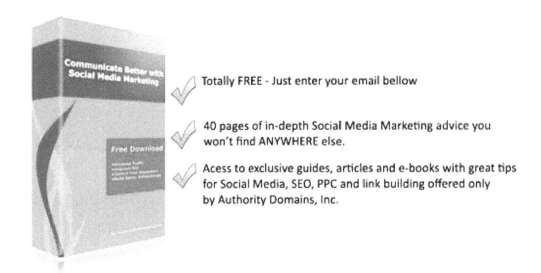

Totally FREE - Just enter your email bellow

40 pages of in-depth Social Media Marketing advice you won't find ANYWHERE else.

Acess to exclusive guides, articles and e-books with great tips for Social Media, SEO, PPC and link building offered only by Authority Domains, Inc.

This is what a great Free Bait banner looks like.

This is how I market my Free Bait before each YouTube video.

It's a bit redundant to say but in-case you don't know, I use BlueHost to host all of my domains in the last 5 years or so. They have great prices and better customer support than any other customer support I ever got from any company, ever. Couldn't recommend more highly, here is the link: https://goo.gl/P0Dlsg.

Free Bait: Once the person clicked on the link to your bait he'll reach a Squeeze Page, a Squeeze Page is a web page whose only purpose is to get someone's email address (no menu, header, footer, nothing! Only the offer, keep them focused, it's "give your email or leave"). This guide isn't about using email marketing but as I've said before - even if you don't plan to use them right now, gather as many as possible. In the near future when you'll start doing email marketing, every email you collect now will be worth $1 to $5+ every month. So if you collect 3,000 emails would eventually be worth anywhere between $3,000 to $15,000+ **PER MONTH**. Collect the fucking emails OK? (I personally use GetResponse, it's overall the best email marketing software in-terms of price and ease of use. This is the link: https://goo.gl/k7iAwu, you should bookmark it for later).

There are many types of Squeeze Pages (some examples below), the one you should stick to is the Long Squeeze Page (you can find many examples by searching Google Images for "Long Squeeze Page"). My homepage (www.robbyfrank.com) is also a Long Squeeze Page. The reason I like those the most is because they are very detailed and really tell the story of who you are and what you can do while offering a fantastic conversion rate (about 50% for "cold"/advertising traffic and 70% for "warm"/organic traffic). If you're going to start using Robby's Sales Funnel you should always use a Long Squeeze Page.

If you need help in making them I recommend you try ClickFunnels. You can literally build FULL sales funnel in just 10 minutes. This is the link: https://goo.gl/pKhwOr, you should bookmark it for later.

This is a simple popup Squeeze Page.

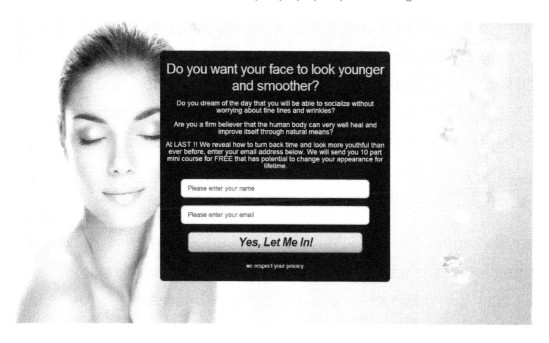

This is a scammy-looking Squeeze Page, still works though.

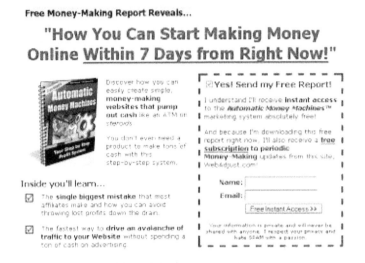

This is a classic "Make Money Online" Squeeze Page.

Free Consultation: This is where it gets juicy, after people are "warmed up" by the free gift and leaving their email, you basically "upsell" them in the momentum of action to take <u>another</u> action that's a lot more valuable to you. This is because it's much easier to ask someone to do something small, and then something bigger, than just asking him to do the bigger thing right-off-the-bat. Expect about a 20% conversion of people trying to <u>qualify</u> for a free strategy session / consultation call.

The reason I stress the word "qualify" is because we're not going to let everyone though the gates, remember the 3 characteristics of a client from Step 2? We want only people who 1. Are VERY interested, 2. Are financially solid, and 3. You'll get-along with.

You don't need to go crazy with the design, as I've said - ClickFunnels will take GOOD care of you and do it for you in 5 minutes, you just need to take care of filling the chosen template with content.

I've included a few good examples for free consultation application pages:

http://www.donovanrussell.com/free-consultation.html

https://www.clearadmit.com/services/free-consultation/

https://www.newbreedmarketing.com/free-consultation

All 3 are great examples, obviously there are better examples, but there are also worse. These will do just fine.

The only thing you must remember if you want to give yourself a real easy time is to qualify, this is how I recommend to qualify the 3 characteristics:

Interest: "How long have you been interested in _____?", "How much time per ____ day you practice _____", "Have you invested in books / courses / seminars etc.. for this subject?".

Financially (Either ask indirectly or just straight up ask): "Have you invested in ____ before?", "Are you able to afford _____".
(You can write "we occasionally offer scholarships for underprivileged applicants" below the "are you able to afford" question, this is a very strong incentive to get people who can't / can barely afford your products to be honest about their financial situation. Not to sound mean but that's a great way to filter out the poor and struggling people, with some exceptions of-course.)

Affinity (Ask questions that require a long/personal response): "What are your values/goals for _____", "what are you looking to achieve in the next _____", "How do you think I can help you?".

Out of the applications you get, only about a third would actually qualify in-terms of what we are looking for (very interested, has money, great chemistry), this is only if you want REALLY high quality consultation calls with very high closing ratios.

Now, the actual consultation call.

The Consultation Call: First and foremost, <u>I don't want you to think of this as a sales call</u>. When I do a free coaching call I don't spend a single moment stressing about money, closing or anything of that sort. The way I start the call is by really getting to know the person and just helping them as much as possible in the 30 minutes to 3 hours I'm going to spend with that person on the phone (Skype call to be precise).

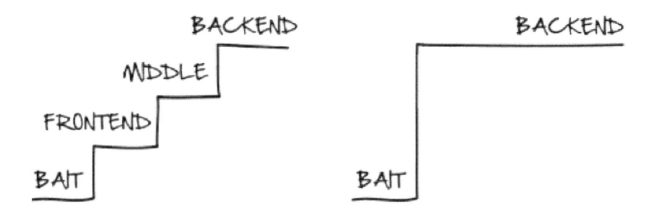

If you recall the value ladder the entire point of it is to get someone to invest in you, then give them back more value; once you've given enough value you can progress up the steps and get that person to invest more value in you, rinse - repeat.

What we're doing with this consultation call is to give so much value that we can skip straight to the top of the ladder and close the $1,000+ sale.

This means that your job isn't to be a salesman, be pushy, be scammy, or whatever you might think it is. Your job is to give so much value to the other person that by the end of the call HE will ask YOU how much your product or service costs and if HE'S good enough and qualifies to work with YOU.

The more you can make the call exactly like the actually product / service the more likely it is that the person will want to buy. So if you're selling a course for example, all you need to do is give a passionate taste of the course by giving a demonstration of a lesson or two in the course.

Give the person as much value as he needs to make a decision, this is why my calls last from 30 minutes to 3 full hours (and I enjoy every moment of them), obviously if you don't enjoy the call for any reason feel free to make it short or just finish it on the spot. I took this into account when I wrote the 20% closing rate figure in the Robby's Sales Funnel table.

Same if you're a coach trying to close $1,000+ customers, simply coach the person exactly as you would if he were your client already, don't even think about selling, you'll know intuitively what's the exact perfect time to transition into closing the deal, just like you know intuitively when to kiss a boy or a girl.

Obviously when you sense that the person got enough value and wants to make a decision, there are some logistics you want to take care of, don't shy away from the following questions towards the end:

- "How much did this session help you / teach you?"
- "Feel free to refer any friend you have that is like you and also needs a coaching session / might consider joining."
- "Do you like what you got so far? Would you like to go for the full coaching / course / payment ?"
- "Do you want to purchase / join or is there anything that's stopping you from doing it?"
- "How does the offer sound?"

When you're at this point of the call, simply apply common sense and don't overthink things. Things are as they seem. If the person sounds a bit nervous or uncertain, honestly ask him what's bothering him, if the person doesn't sound interested, just ask him if it doesn't seem like a good fit, and of course, if the person does sound interested, just tell him you'd love to work with him or add him to the course and see what happens.

At this stage I had many cool things happen, sometimes people think you're worth $2,000 when you were about to ask for $1,000, just say "great!" and close the $2,000 deal. I've also had people tell me that they're nervous about investing all that money, so I just closed them on doing another call, this time for $150 per hour. So play around with it, be creative, focus on giving value that matches what you're trying to sell, and have fun!

Step 4. Business Automation

In this segment we're going to focus on marketing and creating automatic traffic for your sales funnel. As we've discussed in Step 3, once you've built your funnel the most precious thing you can get is traffic, traffic and more traffic, since the more traffic you get, the more money you make.

Obviously you don't want to always be working all day and you want to be able to not work and still see the sales funnel working for you.

I have some friends that do internet marketing and make more than $3,000 per day but because they had too much pride to automate certain things early they're now stuck in a loop of working 14+ hours per day keeping their monster business going but never having time to back off, relax, or create a system that automatically takes care of these parts of the business.

With that quick caveat out of the way, let's start breaking down the different ways that you can build systems that automate your business. Remember that the goal is to create a business that makes a ton of money for you <u>and gives you freedom</u>.

Keep in mind before we begin that while some solutions are free, some will cost you money (ideally a tiny percentage of your revenue), don't start automating parts of the business that you could do yourself before you see revenue.

Remember: <u>The 2 reasons to automate parts of your sales funnel are to create space for more growth and to make sure the business never controls you. How do you know if your business controls you? When you can't always choose what to do with your time.</u>

There are 3 types of "automation" solutions that you can use to make your business as passive as possible:

- **Employee Automation:** Paying someone to do something.
- **Paid Automation:** Paying something to do something.
- **Passive Automation:** Getting something to do something for free.

The easiest way to understand what needs automation is always to go back to your sales funnel. Remember, anytime you're having trouble selling, not seeing enough results, or anytime you want to automate, change or improve something about the business, always go back to your sales funnel and use the statistics and broad view of things to see where the problem is and what you can do about it.

Anytime you need to diagnose a business, whether it's yours or someone else's, draw a table and start identifying the sales funnel from the traffic, to the bait, to the Front End (low-ticket), Middle (mid-ticket) and Back End (high ticket) parts of the business.

Let's bring back our special high-ticket sales funnel and start identifying how we can basically automate every part of the funnel, and what happens if we don't automate it:

Robby's Sales Funnel	Statistics
Monthly Traffic	1,000
Free Bait (50%)	500
Free Consultation (20%)	100
Qualify For Call (33%)	33
$1497 Sale (20%)	6.6
Total Income	**$9,880**

As you can see our sales funnel gets a traffic of about 1,000 monthly visitors, half of them give their emails at the Free Bait / Squeeze Page, then a fifth sign up to a free consultation, and a third qualify for the actual call.

The best way to identify what should get automated is to hypothetically multiply the results of 10x every step and see what happens:

If we get 10,000 monthly traffic instead of 1,000 that means 5,000 people will give their emails - that's automatic, so no problem there..

Automation Solution Example 1:

Out of 5,000 people about 1,000 are going to apply to our consultation call every month, that could be a problem! I don't want to look at 33 different forms every day of the month! That would be exhausting and boring, I did not create a business to do this stupid shit, so let's see how we can automate this using the 3 different automation solutions:

- **Employee Automation:** You can pay someone to look at the different applications and teach them how to sort them out, you can easily hire freelancers online from 3rd world countries to do it for you professionally for just $10 per hour.
- **Paid Automation:** I don't believe there's any computer or online service that can automatically do this job, so no ideas here.
- **Passive Automation:** One way to automate the process to some extent would be to create automatic filters based on certain answers. For example, to automatically filter out any application where the person doesn't have the ability to afford our products (using smart questions like those I showed you in Step 3). This way we can filter at-least half the applications. We can also filter all the applications where the answers to certain important questions are shorter than 5 words, this means the person filing the application is lazy, this filters another 20%. So just by setting up a bunch of filters like this (you can easily do this through your Gmail server for example) we essentially filtered our applications to just around 30%, so instead of going through 33 applications per day it's just 10 which takes a couple of

minutes, this means we are well prepared for a situation where we get 10,000 monthly visitors instead of just 1,000.

Automation Solution Example 2:

If we have 1,000 different monthly applications, and we only talk to about 30% of them, that means we're going to have 300 free consultation calls per month (and about 60 monthly sales, so around $90,000 per month   ), 300 consultation calls means 10 calls every day which is logistically impossible since every call is between 30 minutes to 3 hours (trust me, I've tried).

We could always just make these a "group consultation call" (an idea I've had for a long time but never tried), but let's stick to the program and see how we can automate this using the 3 different automation solutions:

- **Employee Automation:** Simple, just hire people to sell for you. Pay them based on results, meaning that they only get paid if they make a sale. Give them 10% of the sale ($150) in the form of a PayPal commision. This way you can train and hire ANYONE from ANYWHERE as long as they have the sales skills to match. I have a friend that sells a $3,000 course and at any given time has between 2 to 5 people selling full times for him based on commissions only, he simply offers people who take his course the opportunity to sell for him and trains the ones that qualify. *There's nothing like selling high-ticket products and having a huge pie of income in every sale that you can cut small pieces of to motivate people to work for you while taking none of the risk since it's based on results only!*
- **Paid Automation:** You can pay a remote sales force company that basically closes these sales for you. I would highly recommend that

you stay away from outsourcing the sales of your high-ticket items and always keep it in house.

- **Passive Automation:** The only way to passively automate a sales process for a high-ticket product is by creating an automated system giving people <u>so much value</u> (comparable to your one-on-one call) that they'll naturally move up to the high-ticket product without you being there. The best way you can do this is using a video-series launch format, this is a process where you sign someone up to a free mini-course usually composed of 4 free videos. Every day you let the user watch another video with each video gradually hitting more and more "mental triggers" that get people to want to buy things, then on the 4th video you offer your course for anywhere from $997 up to $7999 or more, at this point you gave so much free value and built up so much expectation that many people convert and buy the high-ticket course right then and there.

PRODUCT LAUNCH FUNNEL

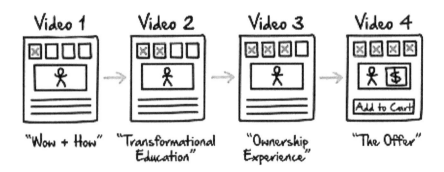

This is how a passive high-ticket sales process usually looks.

Automation Solution Example 3:

The final automation example I'll give relates to traffic, marketing and getting traffic is another part of your business that you want to automate as much as possible. I mainly use my YouTube videos for marketing, but I love putting out daily content, it is part of my freedom and fun, and if I don't upload for a day or two it only creates expectation and the traffic makes up for my down-time, along with the passive YouTube traffic I get every day no matter what just because I have so many videos online. And of-course my automatic email newsletter that gets sent out daily to all my subscribers, all pre-made.

Getting traffic using automation:

- **Employee Automation:** You can hire people to create and upload content for you on YouTube, FaceBook, Blogs, Forums etc.. Anything to get your Free Bait out there to the right people. I've even gone so far as to hire someone to send messages to people from specific Facebook groups for me using my profile and a script I gave him to generate free consultation calls for me. He would offer to send people one of my free 1+ hour videos. Most people would agree to watch it (they invest in me), then they would watch the 1+ hour video (they get some value from me), then he would ask them if they want a free coaching call, some would say "yes" (they invest in me), then I'd give them a ton of value and try to close them on the phone with about 20% closing rate. This was a solution that basically completely automated traffic for me, leaving me to just do the coaching and keep about 85% of the $10k income..

- **Paid Automation:** This solution is all about paying for advertising. Your main tool would be Facebook ads. Advertising has vastly changed over the last few years and there's no one I could recommend more highly to learn Facebook Ads from then my friend Ben Malol who's making well over a $1,000,000 a year in sales from Facebook Ads and also teaches people how to do it too, you can easily find him on google, he also has the biggest Facebook Ads Group in the world with 30,000+ members, you can check it out with this link: https://goo.gl/hVstxn.

- **Passive Automation:** The best way to use passive automation for your traffic is to simply create content that has long-term sustainability. The more content you create the more assets you'll have to bring you passive traffic. I personally recommend creating daily content (articles, videos, blog posts, forum posts, group's comments) for at-least 2-3 months before moving to more passive or paid types of traffic, just make sure everything you do includes your Bait! That's the key component of your marketing. Every single piece of content you put out should always serve 2 goals: to give people value, and to use that value to get them to click on your Free Bait offer.

Step 4. Summary:

- The 2 reasons to automate parts of your sales funnel are to create space for more growth and to make sure the business never controls you.
- How do you know if your business controls you? When you can't always choose what to do with your time.
- Any "inspection" of your business starts with laying out your sales funnel from traffic, to Free Bait, all the way to the biggest sale.
- Use your sales funnel to identify where your business needs more automation, multiply your stats by 10x to see what part of the sales funnel will be a future problem if it's not eventually automated.
- Analyze and think of automation solutions for parts of your sales funnel using the 3 types of automation - Passive, Employee and Paid.
- Always be aware which parts of the sales funnel will need automating in the future, if you track which parts of your business will need automating when it grows, it will limit its growth potential.
- Remember, don't spend money and time automating things that don't actually need automation at the moment - stay frugal and automate parts of your sales funnel only to nurture more growth and freedom.
- Every single piece of content you put out should always serve 2 goals: to give people value, and to use that value to get them to click on your Free Bait offer.

Step 5. Common Pitfalls & Mistakes

Many people will gladly tell you all about "the 5 top mistakes that you do while trying to achieve XYZ" (usually well trying to sell you a product that fixes it).

It's not often though that you hear someone talk about what not to do, or the top X mistakes people make when they become successful at something.

At this point in my life I could've easily bought a new Ferrari or Lamborghini just with the money I would've saved I had someone call me to avoid them earlier.

The type of money I did you to make here is on one hand how many much bigger than you've ever made but also can be attained within a couple of months.

This type of quick change of life situation usually results in very poor decision-making, the reason for that is that you carry with you the mentality of a regular person but have the self-esteem and income have a very successful person.

Match that with the fact that I am an absolute maniac/retard and you get a recipe for a beautiful disaster.

No add onto that and the fact that I'm also fairly talented, and can maneuver my way out of really dumb situations, and you actually get a feedback loop where the crazier I get in the more risks I take, the more my followers cheer and support me and the more money I seem to make.

So to summarize, when people quickly jump to a much higher income bracket been before, they tend to make really bad decisions.

This is the point of this chapter, I want you to avoid those decisions which would save you a lot of money, save you from trauma and regret, and allow you to continually grow your business and seeing your income increase in even more.

I can boil down the biggest mistakes you can make it to the following categories:

1. Changing Your Original Environment:

> Always remember that until the point that you became successful, you were not successful. When I mean by this is that something has triggered a change in your thinking that created your success, this may be a mentor, successful friend, or even a really good book or YouTube channel.

> When you experience a sudden surge of success at first you may be very thankful to that thing or person, but as time goes on and your self-esteem increases you're very likely to start believing that "you had it in you all along", or that "just a special kind of breed", or the worst - "it's just who I am now".

> I am member first experiencing this mistake after a Europe tour I had. I was visiting my home country of Israel for 3 to 4 months and basically cut ties with my previous mentor.

In another words, I was the most successful person that I knew personally at the time.

After hearing "Oh my god you're amazing! How do you make so much money!" Etc. I started actually feeling like maybe I am making a lot of money, closing clients became a lot harder, my creative growth ideas all but dissipated and my business growth halted to a crawl.

The moment I left back to Europe and got back in contact with highly successful people (or more importantly, stop being in contact with people who are not successful) it immediately felt like a breath of fresh air.. All of my ambition, imagination and passion came back. It's like when you're in a weird haze and then you can suddenly think straight again, that's literally how it feels like.

Also, the more successful people you are influenced by are the faster your success will increase in the bigger you're thinking will be.

A lot of my current progress happened because I got back in touch with a couple of friends of mine or making millions of dollars of our year online.

I was actually pretty content with things and happy with just coaching people for $3,000 per client, and then I met a friend of mine that makes what I makes $3,000 every day passively just from selling online courses.

2. Trying to Impress People:

Another big mistake I made was trying way too hard to let people know just how successful and famous I am. I would throw out huge tips, rent places for $5,000+ even when that was 75% of what I was making, eat morning, afternoon and night at restaurants, and take luxury taxis anywhere I go.

This might seem like it has nothing to do with you because you'll never act this dumb, but there are a lot of people I've met including me that did.

The root cause of that I believe is trying to make-up for a lack of self-esteem, having a background feeling of not being enough just by being yourself.

Keep in mind that using money to fill this void is a bottomless pit, and the people that will give you validation for it are the exact type of people you don't want in your life right now (gulible, low self-esteem, no financial understanding etc..).

To make this point even more clear, the same followers and fans I had when things were amazing and I was making a ton of money (and spending a ton of money), are the same people that disappeared the instant I went into my first personal/business crisis.

Those same people that tell you now how amazing you are are the ones who are going to tell everybody what a jackass you are the moment you stop filling their need do you have someone to idolize (meaning, "more than human").

It's actually the people that are telling you that you're acting like a retard that you should listen to.

Ironically, when you're on the drug of validation it's highly unlikely that you'll listen to these people, you'll just think that they don't "get it".

Remember, be the silent but impressive silverback gorilla, the one that grabs attention just by being, not the small barking dog that wants everyone to pay attention to him. Let your success speak for itself, the important people will notice, and the shit ones won't.

3. Spending Before Saving:

To quote Warren Buffet, "DO NOT SAVE WHAT IS LEFT AFTER SPENDING, BUT SPEND WHAT IS LEFT AFTER SAVING."

When you start seeing big sales coming in, take it one step at a time and I don't start spending the money. I know it sounds weird and you're asking yourself why the hell would you do that, but when you've just close the $2000 sale, after making $2000 a month for the last few years, you tend to believe that this is just the way it's going to be now and are you going to make this kind of sale every day or every week.

When you do get to that point of closing $1000 or more per sale every couple of days, remember to save about 80% of it for investing in your business and only use 20% or less for leisure and fun.

I would often find myself spending about 70% or more of the money I get from every sale, the biggest reason was that I was super confident in my ability to generate income and knew that I would make another sale very soon.

This would often lead to things like me flying somewhere, booking an extremely expensive house or apartment, and living large no matter what, even while my money was starting to run out.

The worst that got for me was actually signing contracts upfront for things I didn't have money to, I would sign contracts for $10,000, $20,000 and sometimes more where I agreed to pay the money by a certain time, this created a ton of stress and instead of focusing on growing my business I would always be focusing on that next sale that would pay for the thing I have a deadline for.

But the truth is, the worst part wasn't just the stress, it was saying business opportunities that I could've easily grab, and not being able to afford them because I just spent most of my money on consumables, renting, and other things that come as fast as they disappear.

So to summarize, from the first moment you close $1000 or more on your first sale, celebrate, take out $200 or more depending on how much you closed, use that money to celebrate and put the remaining $800 or more on the side for the sole purpose of investing in your business to get more of these amazing sales.

4. Emotional decision making:

I'm a very, very passionate guy and I don't care too much about money, at least not as much as I care about doing something I really love, so this one was most likely the hardest for me.

What I mean by emotional decision making is that you let your mind and emotions dictate your life to the level that if you suddenly get an urge to quit the business, to change it, or anything of the sort, you'll often listen to the urge even if it doesn't make any sense.

You'll know if this error applies to you if you've ever done one of the following:

1. Quit a job immediately and without previous notice.
2. Quit a relationship immediately and without previous notice.
3. Made a very important life decision in one moment without really thinking about it.

These are examples of actions that someone with a very emotion-based decision-making would do.

This doesn't mean that you don't justify your actions later using logic and rationalizations, what it means is that at the time of making the decision the main factor was the fact that you really really felt like it.

Unfortunately for me, I've probably made more stupid decisions in my life just because I really felt like doing them then I have good decisions because they were the right thing to do.

One example that actually happened multiple times for me was me having kind of an uninspired few days, you know, those days where you just don't feel like it.

Anyway, I was working with clients, and making over $2,500 a week, but because I felt uninspired for a few days I just sat in front of my desk and in a rush of inspiration felt like I should do something else, so I just told all my clients and I'm stopping the coaching for now, gave out refunds, deleted my YouTube and website, basically – did something really really dumb.

As I've said, this happened multiple times to me, with different businesses and every time I had to start from scratch.

While I can't stop you from making such a hasty decision (and if you've identified with one of the examples above, trust me this might just be you), I could advise you that at least you never destroy or delete anything that you created.

I know that you like to identify with "the new you", but trust me, anything you've built whether it's a product, a sales funnel, a YouTube channel or another form of content, it's never worth destroying even if you don't identify with it anymore.

Either let it live out and just be there in the case of something like a YouTube channel, or find a way to preserve whatever it is you made like a website or something so that you'll always have access to it in the future.

So again, do you emotional types out there, hear me out — never destroy anything you created, preserve everything, you'll never know when you'll need it.

Also remember, success always takes time. You need to grow anything that you want to have an abundance, and again that takes time.

If something like a couple of bad days is enough to deter you from your current destination and convince you to start something new entirely, the odds that it will happen again are very very big. So instead of being in a constant cycle of building a destroying shit, try sticking to something as if you're married to it and see what happens.

One final point, your business isn't make to make you happy, just like your relationship isn't meant to make you happy, just like your friends are not meant to make you happy.

You could try relying on those to make you happy, but anything external that you're relying on in life is bound to disappoint you at some point.

While you're building your business also build a foundation of inner peace, not being dragged up and down by the current external situation, that way, if you have a really bad month in terms of sales, that doesn't affect you on a deep level, and also if you have a really good month in terms of sales, that doesn't pull you up to cloud nine in terms of happiness only to slam you down the moment things go wrong.

5. Taking success for granted:

I talked about this briefly in a few of the other mistakes but this mistake is so important that I have to reiterate it here specifically.

What you have to understand is that the "you" that you think you are isn't actually who you are.

What I mean by this is that you're actually "nothing", or to be more precise you are even less than nothing, this is because everything about "you" that you value so much and identify as yourself, is actually created because of your external environment.

Basically, all of your thoughts, opinions, beliefs and drives were things that you soaked up like a sponge overtime based on your external environment.

Just because you created a successful online business and are now making more money than almost anyone you know doesn't mean that you have changed as a person "forever".

If you look closely, you'll see that your success is the result of putting yourself around as many successful influences as possible and also away from unsuccessful influences as much as possible.

So now that you have a business that successful, you probably have a very high-level thinking and everything about success just makes sense.

I dare you to try though, moving away from your success influences (mentor, books, friends etc.) and see just how long that high level of thinking stays.

As I previously stated, I have made every single mistake you could possibly make and so, I'll share with you on a personal level, what happened to me relating to this mistake.

Never mind the many times I surrounded myself with unsuccessful people after I became successful thinking that it doesn't matter because that's just who I am now and then found out later that my thinking level and motivation or quickly dropping.

The main thing I want to share with you is a very dark. That happened to me a year ago where I entered into a few months of a deep depression due to events that you have to read about in Evolution of a Maniac.

During my depression I wasn't coaching anyone and so I wasn't making any money, I decided to go back to the city where my parents live and stay near them, and for a few months I was basically either with them or out alone taking walks.

My parents aren't particularly successful, that actually just your average family in terms of income.

After these 2−3 months of being almost entirely influenced by them and my immediate environment, I lost about 99% of all my high-level thoughts about business, $1000 seems like a lot of money to me (when just a few months later I was making up to $15,000 a month), and I even found myself thinking about doing some freelance work like your average person instead of just getting back on the horse and making five figure monthly income again.

Luckily, I have a really good connections with some highly successful people that I reached out and pulled me out of that low level thinking regarding business.

So just remember, your influences dictate who you are; not in the deepest level of coarse, but in the way that most people consider their identity (again, I referred to thinking, beliefs etc.).

If you hang out with people that make over $1,000,000 a year, The odds that you'll also make close to that much or more are very high. Either way, you'll definitely be gravitating towards that much money.

On the other hand, if you aim to make $1,000,000 a year but almost everyone you know makes less than $70,000 a year, and you don't have a single friend or mentor that makes that much, the odds of you getting even close to it or almost 0.

Before pursuing any goal, get to know someone who's gone way beyond what you're aiming for and you'll get there 10 times faster than you thought you could and increase your success chance from almost 0 to a very high number.

6. Becoming an arrogant ass:

As I've said, I've made every possible mistake you could think of ha ha.

Just to give you a funny example one of the friends I told you about that makes over $3000 a day, was actually a friend of mine from age 18 who found his success only AFTER I became successful myself.

And so, and his desire to become more successful with me being the only successful person he knew, he reached out to me to sit with him for an hour or two and give them a few tips.

My head was so far deep into my ass that I arrive to the meeting with the luxury suit, and talked to him for that hour with a tone of "I'm so important and you should be grateful for even speaking to me right now".

And as if that was not bad enough, if you weeks later while I was traveling in Europe he sent me a Facebook message, the conversation went something like this:

Ben - "Hey man, how are you doing?"

Me - "Fine."

Ben - "Are you in Israel or Europe?"

Me - "That's a stupid question."

Ben - "So Europe..?"

Me - "I don't have time for stupid questions like this."

That's how the conversation went, I was quite a jackass.

So remember not to be an ass because those people that you're disrespecting could be the same people that will help you somewhere along the way.

And also, I guess that all the shit I went through was sort of karma getting back at me for being a dick.

Lesson learned :-)

7. Being Consumed By Business:

I left out the final mistake to the end, this is just a horrible, horrible thing that happens to almost everyone when they first find success.

The thing is, when you're not successful and you don't make money, it's very easy to stop focusing on the business (also because you almost certainly have no one who's successful at that area as part of your life).

Once you actually get the ball rolling and see some level of success, it's very easy to get completely sucked into the business, do you feel that strong anxiety feeling that tells you you have to do more, think more, and not miss anything so that the ball keeps rolling.

I'm all for taking action and also planning ahead, what I'm not for is doing it out of anxiety and fear that you'll lose what you have.

You may not feel it so strongly if you build your success very gradually, but while we're talking about here in this Blueprint is how to jump from nothing to making $1000+ sales.

This is unlike almost anything else I have experience in life, because it really felt like I was finally doing something amazing.

Most people, just like me, I have a ton of baggage linked to two things, first is women (or men, depending on your preference), and the second is money.

Everything from my dream car, to social status, to being able to take care of my parents, to being able to "impress" girls, to the low self-esteem I had and how having a lot of money was supposed to change that, and more.

And so, jump in quickly to making a lot of money triggered a very bad side of my personality, very proud one but a very fearful one, that's why I couldn't stop thinking about the business, and that's why I was so full of anxiety all day long.

This mistake of being run by that anxiety about your business has actually lead to most of the mistakes I've listed above.

Because of that anxiety I was constantly changing my environment because I was trying to run away from that feeling of being drained.

Because of that anxiety I was constantly trying to impress people with my money and success. This was my ego trying to justify why all that stress was worth it.

Because of that anxiety I was spending a lot of money instead of investing it, because when your run by stress you always feel a sense of lack and need that is actually very easy to fill up very temporarily when you have a lot of disposable income.

Because of that anxiety I was making very emotional decisions, when you feel so rundown and stressed all the time it's very easy to reach that point we just say "fuck it" and just jump ship and try something else entirely.

Because of that anxiety I tried convincing myself that success is just part of me now and that I can't lose that way of thinking anymore. This was obviously a lie built to cover up the anxiety of facing the fact that the world is always changing and that you never know what could happen or how you're thinking could change based on your life situation.

And finally, because of that anxiety I became a serious ass because I was honestly afraid of anyone who wasn't as successful as me but it wasn't a client, I felt as if anyone less successful than me was somehow "contagious" and will lower my level of thinking gradually to his or hers. While on some level this is true, the fact that I had such strong anxiety about it was the actual problem, not other people.

All of these mistakes could be summed: up by one thing, being overly identified with your mind.

Step 5. Summary:

On one hand I'm sorry this chapter a drag for so long, but on another I'm happy I've been able to summarize to the best of my ability the biggest mistakes I've made that I've caused me the most money and heartache.

Make sure you go through this list again the moment you make your first sale, it's going to seem redundant and you probably won't want to do it (kind of like how you don't want to do something boring when you're in a really, really good mood).

And with that, this concludes the five steps of this blueprint to creating an amazing lifestyle where you get to travel and make a lot of money while doing it :-)

Conclusion

I'd like to start this conclusion by thanking my Mom and Dad. Just kidding.

I'd like to start this conclusion by telling you that if you got this far, that means you're a person that I would probably love very much to know; and not just because you were able to bear through the long writing and horrible diction, it's because anyone who got this far is receptive to the type of thinking that got me and my most successful friends to where we are at.

Well I might not end up being that friend or mentor that you need to find, I would like you to let me know if you have any questions or any setback that you need help with.

If I had someone successful that I felt comfortable talking to you whenever I went through any problem, I guarantee you I would not of made even 5% of the mistakes I made an would've probably been 10x more successful than I am today (I do have those successful people in my life today by the way).

If you haven't done so already, please join my Facebook group called "Ask Robby Anything". The group was built specifically for the purpose of having a way for people to ask me questions where I can answer them publicly so that other people could benefit as well.

Now, regarding the tools that I've been using to host my website and send you my email, as well as the tool every single one of my marketing friends used to build sales funnels, these are the links:

Website & Domain Hosting:

> I use BlueHost for all of my domains for over 5 years now. They have great prices and better customer support than any other customer support I ever got from any company, ever

Email Marketing:

> I use GetResponse because it's overall the best email marketing software in-terms of price and ease of use. Highly recommended for anyone with a list of 500 emails or more.

Building Sales Funnels:

> I personally don't use ClickFunnels because I like to build websites manually, every friend I have that makes over $1,000,000 a year uses

And so, we reached the end of the Blueprint. I believe you have everything you could need in terms of practical business models and knowledge to meet you almost any financial goal, especially the simple and easy goal of closing your first $1000+ sale.

I'd start by mapping out who are the people that you'd like to serve, what is the best result you can give them, and with that expensive product is.

From there, go step-by-step through the business model I presented to you in Step 3 and map out your funnel.

If you were planning on selling a course I recommend that you start by coaching people one-on-one because that's the best way to organize your knowledge and make sure that you know how to pass it on.

Once you have mapped out your funnel simply create your bait, use click funnels if you'd like to automatically create the sales funnel or alternatively use BlueHost to purchase at the main and build a website yourself.

Remember that whenever you face a setback and it feels like things are moving forward you can always identify the problem easily just by looking at your funnel. Your problems always come down to either not having a funnel, not converting enough in one or more steps of the final (use examples in Step 3 as benchmark for conversion rates), or finally, simply not having enough traffic to reach to the final step of the funnel.

Thank you for reading this blueprint, I hope you'll put it into action. I'm aware that when we get free shit we tend to not appreciate it as much, which is why I also offer my full life story, as an "origin story" to Robby Frank and do everything that I teach.

I highly recommend that you get it in the next page, and I've even offered you an exclusive discount just because I want to give you a extra motivation to invest in yourself even more.

I'll finish this with the you saw in the first page of my website:

"Inner peace & enthusiastic action lead to the best of all outcomes"

Remember that your inner purpose is to find peace in every moment, while your outer purpose to achieve whatever it is you want at the moment.

Never take this journey too seriously, it's actually when you take a step back and enjoy the ride that the positive things will suddenly (almost magically) begin to happen in your life.

CPSIA information can be obtained
at www.ICGtesting.com
Printed in the USA
LVHW062330090722
723127LV00009B/335

Grade 2 Piano

Improve your scales!

Paul Harris

Introduction

Scales and arpeggios *are* important. And if taught and learned imaginatively, they can be fun!

Improve Your Scales! is designed to help you approach scale learning methodically and thoughtfully. Its intention is to turn learning scales into a pleasant, positive and relevant experience by gradually building up the skills to play them through cumulative and enjoyable activities.

What *Improve Your Scales!* is about

The idea of *Improve Your Scales!* is to present you with lots of engaging activities that lead up to playing the scale (and arpeggio). Actually playing the scale is the last thing that you do! These activities build up an understanding (of the fingering, technical issues, the sound, particular features, sense of key and connections with the pieces that you play) to help make the learning of scales really relevant.

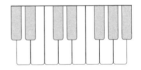

At the top of each scale is a keyboard showing the notes of that particular scale (the minor keys have two keyboards for the melodic minor pattern). This is for you to fill in with whatever you find most useful. Here are some suggestions:
- highlight or colour in the notes of the scale – so you can see the pattern of black and white notes.
- fill in the note names.
- add the fingering you will use for both hands.

Here are two really important **Golden Rules**:

No 1 Before practising your scales make sure that you:
- Drink some water (this helps get the brain working!)
- Relax (especially shoulders, arms, wrists and fingers)
- Check your posture.

No 2 Always practise the scale and arpeggio of the pieces you are learning.

Acknowledgements

Firstly a big thank you to Diana Jackson who, through her considerable and distinguished teaching experience, has furnished many valuable thoughts and ideas.

Thanks also to Claire Dunham whose terrific eye for detail has been invaluable. Also to my own teacher Graeme Humphrey who helped so much in preparing the first edition, and Ann Priestley for many useful comments.

Finally, huge thanks to Lesley Rutherford, my wonderful editor at Faber Music, who always goes well beyond the call of duty.

Fingering made easy!

There are actually only a few fingering patterns used for scales. Once you have these clearly in your mind you'll realise that fingering scales is really easy to master!

Every basic scale (major or minor) has eight notes – but we only have five fingers. So we have to devise simple repetitive patterns that will allow us to play the scales comfortably and fluently. Once you understand the pattern you've virtually learnt to play the scale!

There are no new finger patterns to learn for Grade 2. But now you have to play them 'hands together'.

If you are confident in playing scales with each hand separately, try them hands together slowly and you shouldn't have any problems. It is important to practise scales regularly. Every day if possible! They'll soon become easy to control.

Arpeggios

Arpeggios are introduced in Grade 2. An arpeggio is made up of the 1st, 3rd and 5th notes of the scale (when played together they form a triad and, by adding the octave at the top, the *chord*.)

Here are a two useful points to remember:
- The fingering pattern repeats every three notes – so every octave has the same fingering.
- The fifth finger is only used at the beginning (left hand), the end (right hand) or when changing direction.

Aim to play arpeggios evenly – don't accent the first of every three notes.

G major

Fill in the scale:
(See page 2 for details of how to do this.)

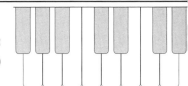

Write the key signature of G major (treble and bass clefs):

The relative minor of G major is: _____

Finger fitness

> **TOP TIP** Play these exercises very slowly at first when you add the second hand.

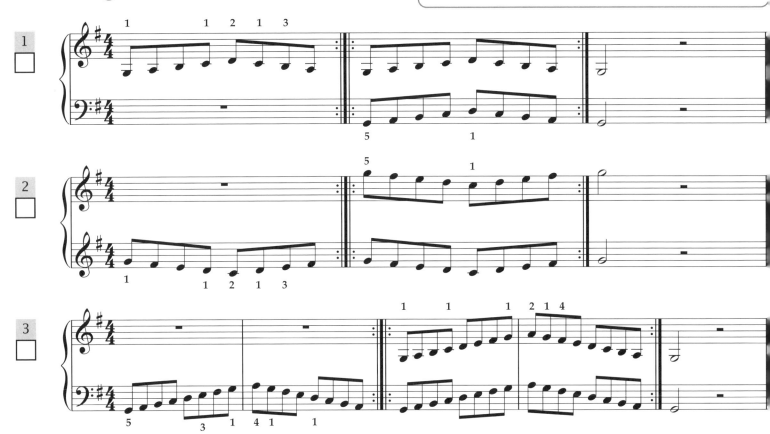

Practise each 2-bar phrase of exercise 4 until it is really under control, then play it complete.

Throughout the book, practise each bar of exercises 5 and 6 separately; then play the whole exercise, repeating it until you are confident and fluent.

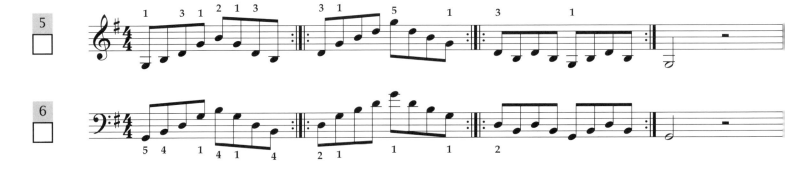

Key piece   Graceful goblins

Allegretto moderato

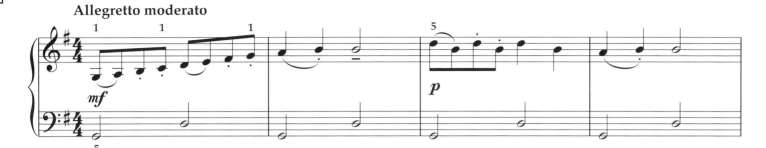

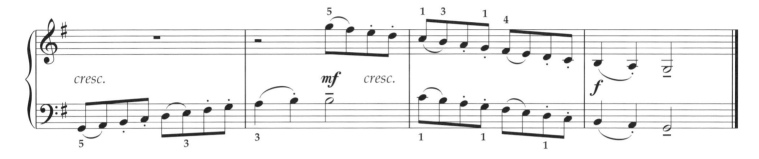

Have a go Using both hands, or just the right-hand line, compose or improvise an answering phrase or a short piece beginning with these notes:

Sight-reading

1 In which key is this piece?

2 Can you spot any repeated patterns?

3 What will you count? Tap the rhythm of each line separately then both lines together.

4 How will you bring character to your performance?

5 Try to hear the music in your head before you begin.

Sprightly

You are now ready to **say** the notes, **hear** the scale or broken chord in your head (playing the key note first), **think** about the fingering and then **play** the scale and arpeggio with confidence!

D major

Fill in the scale:

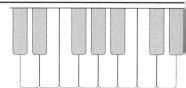

Write the key signature of D major (treble and bass clefs):

The relative minor of D major is: _____

Finger fitness

> **TOP TIP** Always listen carefully to the sound you make.
> Play very carefully so that you never make a mistake.

Key piece   Dainty doughnuts

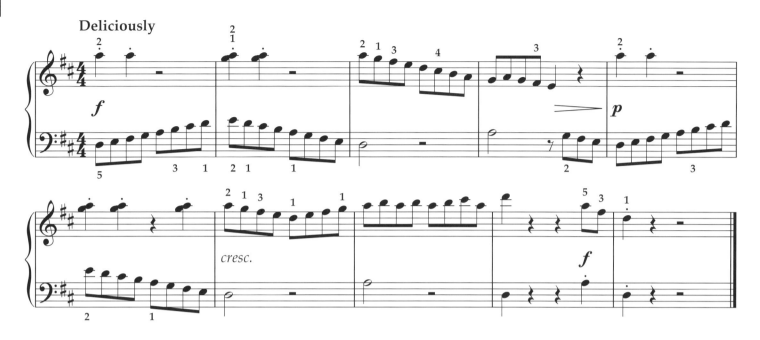

Have a go Using both hands, or just the right-hand line, compose or improvise an answering phrase or a short piece beginning with these notes:

Sight-reading

1 In which key is this piece?

2 Which notes are affected by the key signature?

3 What will you count? Tap the rhythm of each line separately then both lines together.

4 How will you bring character to your performance?

5 Try to hear the music in your head before you begin.

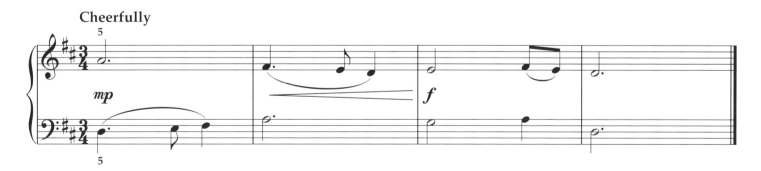

You are now ready to **say** the notes, **hear** the scale or broken chord in your head (playing the key note first), **think** about the fingering and then **play** the scale and arpeggio with confidence!

A major

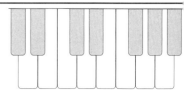

Fill in the scale:

Write the key signature of A major (treble and bass clefs):

Finger fitness

TOP TIP Make sure you control the speed and rhythm when you change direction.

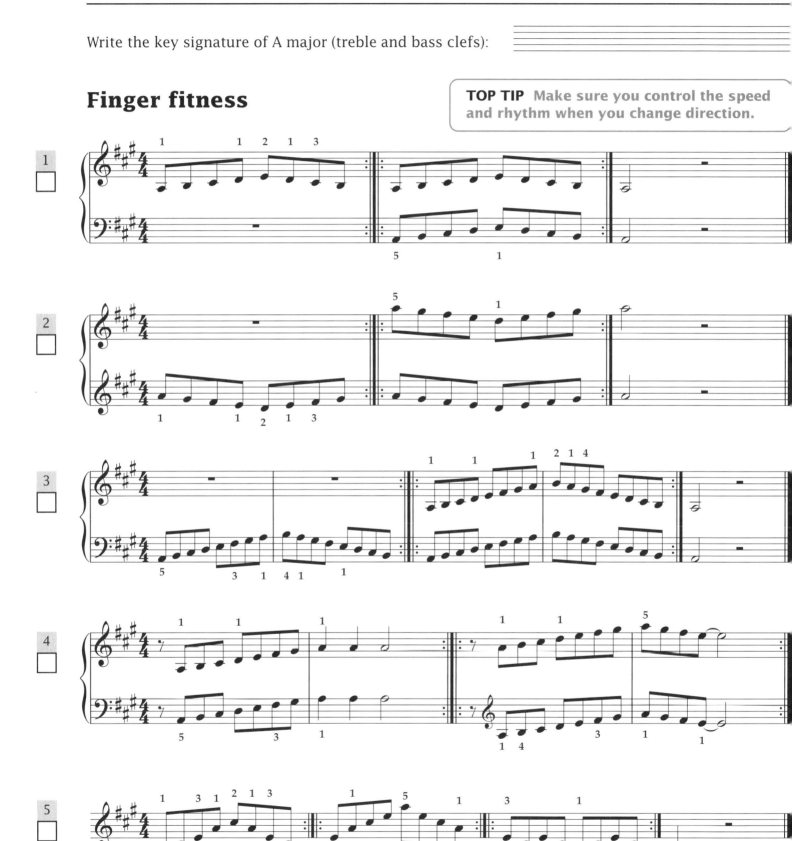

Key piece   Autumn

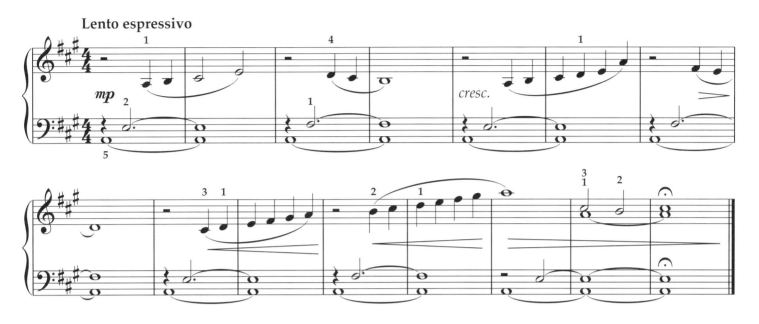

Have a go Using both hands, or just the right-hand line, compose or improvise an answering phrase or a short piece beginning with these notes:

Sight-reading

1   In which key is this piece?
2   Which notes are affected by the key signature?
3   What will you count? Tap the rhythm of each line separately then both lines together.
4   How will you bring character to your performance?
5   Try to hear the music in your head before you begin.

You are now ready to **say** the notes, **hear** the scale or broken chord in your head (playing the key note first), **think** about the fingering and then **play** the scale and arpeggio with confidence!

F major

Fill in the scale:

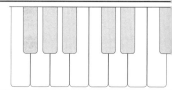

Write the key signature of F major (treble and bass clefs):

The relative minor of F major is: _____

Finger fitness

TOP TIP Notice how thumbs come together in this scale (except when changing direction at the top).

Key piece   Frolic

Have a go Using both hands, or just the right-hand line, compose or improvise an answering phrase or a short piece beginning with these notes:

Sight-reading

1 In which key is this piece?

2 Can you spot any scale or arpeggio patterns?

3 What will you count? Tap the rhythm of each line separately then both lines together.

4 How will you bring character to your performance?

5 Try to hear the music in your head before you begin.

You are now ready to **say** the notes, **hear** the scale or broken chord in your head (playing the key note first), **think** about the fingering and then **play** the scale and broken chord with confidence!

E minor

Fill in the scale:

Write the key signature of E minor:

The relative major of E minor is: _____

Finger fitness

> **TOP TIP** When practising your scales avoid accenting the top note, or landing on the last note with a bump.

1

Harmonic exercises

2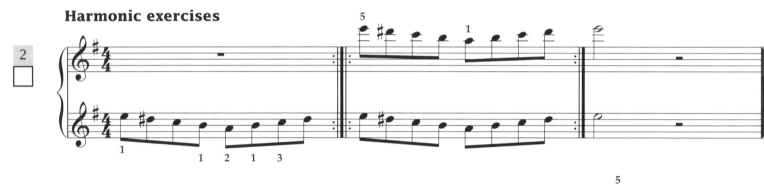

3

4

Broken chord exercises

5

6

Melodic exercises

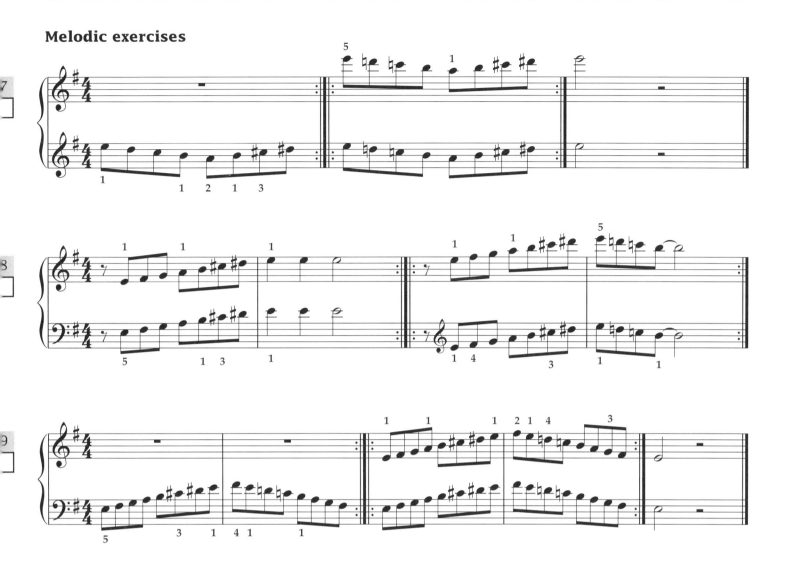

Key piece **Eastern epic** Key piece using E harmonic minor

2

Key piece   **Energetic elf**   Key piece using E melodic minor

3

Have a go   Using both hands, or just the right-hand line, compose or improvise an answering phrase or a short piece beginning with these notes:

4

Sight-reading

1 In which key is this piece?

2 Which notes are affected by the key signature?

3 What should you be particularly careful with, in bar 2 of the left hand?

4 How will you bring character to your performance?

5 Try to hear the music in your head before you begin.

5

You are now ready to **say** the notes, **hear** the scale or broken chord in your head (playing the key note first), **think** about the fingering and then **play** the scale and broken chord with confidence!

Paul Harris' Exam Workout

Improve your sight-reading!

New editions

The ability to sight-read fluently is an important part of musical training, whether intending to play professionally, or simply for enjoyment. By becoming a good sight-reader, the player will be able to learn pieces more quickly, pianists will accompany more easily and all musicians will play duets and chamber music with confidence and assurance. Also, in grade examinations, a good performance in the sight-reading test will result in useful extra marks!

These completely new editions are designed to help incorporate sight-reading regularly into practice and lessons, and to prepare for the sight-reading test in grade examinations. They offer a progressive series of enjoyable and stimulating stages which, with careful work, should result in considerable improvement from week to week.

Step by step, the player is encouraged to build up a complete picture of each piece. Rhythmic exercises help develop and maintain a steady beat, whilst melodic exercises assist in the recognition of melodic shapes at a glance. The study of a prepared piece with associated questions for the student to answer helps consolidate acquired skills and, finally, a series of real, unprepared sight-reading tests in *Going Solo*.

Now available: two *Improve Your Sight-reading!* Piano duet books which give players a chance to practise their sight-reading skills with another player. Carefully paced to be used alongside the rest of the series.

ABRSM Editions

0-571-53300-0	Piano Pre-Grade 1
0-571-53301-9	Piano Grade 1
0-571-53302-7	Piano Grade 2
0-571-53303-5	Piano Grade 3
0-571-53304-3	Piano Grade 4
0-571-53305-1	Piano Grade 5
0-571-53306-X	Piano Grade 6
0-571-53307-8	Piano Grade 7
0-571-53308-6	Piano Grade 8
0-571-52405-2	Duets Grades 0–1
0-571-52406-0	Duets Grades 2–3

Trinity Editions

0-571-53750-2	Piano Grade Initial
0-571-53751-0	Piano Grade 1
0-571-53752-9	Piano Grade 2
0-571-53753-7	Piano Grade 3
0-571-53754-5	Piano Grade 4
0-571-53755-3	Piano Grade 5
0-571-53825-8	Electronic Keyboard Initial–Grade 1
0-571-53826-6	Electronic Keyboard Grades 2–3
0-571-53827-4	Electronic Keyboard Grades 4–5

FABER *ff* MUSIC

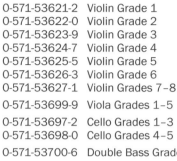
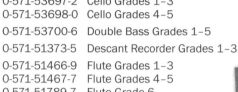

0-571-53621-2	Violin Grade 1
0-571-53622-0	Violin Grade 2
0-571-53623-9	Violin Grade 3
0-571-53624-7	Violin Grade 4
0-571-53625-5	Violin Grade 5
0-571-53626-3	Violin Grade 6
0-571-53627-1	Violin Grades 7–8
0-571-53699-9	Viola Grades 1–5
0-571-53697-2	Cello Grades 1–3
0-571-53698-0	Cello Grades 4–5
0-571-53700-6	Double Bass Grades 1–5
0-571-51373-5	Descant Recorder Grades 1–3
0-571-51466-9	Flute Grades 1–3
0-571-51467-7	Flute Grades 4–5
0-571-51789-7	Flute Grade 6
0-571-51790-0	Flute Grades 7–8
0-571-51464-2	Clarinet Grades 1–3
0-571-51465-0	Clarinet Grades 4–5
0-571-51787-0	Clarinet Grade 6
0-571-51788-9	Clarinet Grades 7–8
0-571-51635-1	Saxophone Grades 1–3
0-571-51636-X	Saxophone Grades 4–5
0-571-51633-5	Oboe Grades 1–3
0-571-57021-6	Oboe Grades 4–5
0-571-51148-1	Bassoon Grades 1–5
0-571-51076-0	Horn Grades 1–5
0-571-50989-4	Trumpet Grades 1–5
0-571-51152-X	Trumpet Grades 5–8
0-571-56860-2	Trombone Grades 1–5

Improve your aural!

New editions

The very thought of aural, especially in examinations, strikes fear into the heart of many young pianists and instrumentalists. But aural should not be an occasional optional extra – it's something to be developing all the time, because having a good ear will help improve musicianship more than any other single musical skill.

Improve your aural! is designed to take the fear out of aural. Through fun listening activities, boxes to fill in and practice exercises, these workbooks and CDs focus on all the elements of the ABRSM aural tests. Because all aspects of musical training are of course connected, the student will also be singing, clapping, playing their instrument, writing music down, improvising and composing – as well as developing that vital ability to do well at the aural test in grade exams!

0-571-53438-4	Grade 1 (with CD)
0-571-53439-2	Grade 2 (with CD)
0-571-53544-5	Grade 3 (with CD)
0-571-53545-3	Grade 4 (with CD)
0-571-53546-1	Grade 5 (with CD)
0-571-53440-6	Grade 6 (with CD)
0-571-53441-4	Grades 7–8 (with CD)

Improve your practice!

Improve your practice! is the essential companion for pianists and instrumentalists, encapsulating Paul Harris's failsafe approach to learning. With boxes for filling in, make-your-own playing cards, a handy practice diary and an exam countdown, these books help to explore pieces and to understand their character. The books will enable the student to develop ways of getting the most out of their practice sessions – whatever their length. Most importantly, the wider musical skills such as aural, theory, sight-reading, improvisation and composition develop alongside, resulting in a more intelligent and all-round musician. Practice makes perfect!

0-571-52844-9	Piano Beginners
0-571-52261-0	Piano Grade 1
0-571-52262-9	Piano Grade 2
0-571-52263-7	Piano Grade 3
0-571-52264-5	Piano Grade 4
0-571-52265-3	Piano Grade 5
0-571-52271-8	Instrumental Grade 1
0-571-52272-6	Instrumental Grade 2
0-571-52273-4	Instrumental Grade 3
0-571-52274-2	Instrumental Grade 4
0-571-52275-0	Instrumental Grade 5

Improve your scales!

Paul Harris's *Improve your scales!* series is the only way to learn scales.

These workbooks contain not only the complete scales and arpeggios for the current ABRSM syllabus but also use finger fitness exercises, scale and arpeggio studies, key pieces and simple improvisations to help you play scales and arpeggios with real confidence.

This unique approach encourages the student to understand and play comfortably within in a key, thus helping them pick up those valuable extra marks in exams, as well as promoting a solid basis for the learning of repertoire and for sight-reading.

0-571-53411-2	Piano Grade 1
0-571-53412-0	Piano Grade 2
0-571-53413-9	Piano Grade 3
0-571-53414-7	Piano Grade 4
0-571-53415-5	Piano Grade 5
0-571-53701-4	Violin Grade 1
0-571-53702-2	Violin Grade 2
0-571-53703-0	Violin Grade 3
0-571-53704-9	Violin Grade 4
0-571-53705-7	Violin Grade 5
0-571-52024-3	Flute Grades 1–3
0-571-52025-1	Flute Grades 4–5
0-571-51475-8	Clarinet Grades 1–3
0-571-51476-6	Clarinet Grades 4–5

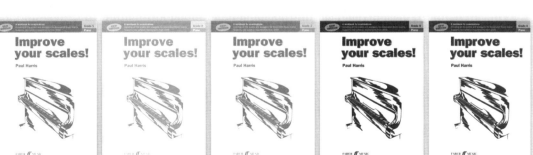

Improve your teaching!

Energising and inspirational, *Improve your teaching!* and *Teaching Beginners* are 'must have' handbooks for all instrumental and singing teachers. Packed full of comprehensive advice and practical strategies, they offer creative yet accessible solutions to the challenges faced in music education.

Group Music Teaching in Practice is a major resource designed to help class teachers, instrumental teachers and music services collaborate and refine their skills to enable them to deliver an holistic primary music curriculum.

These insightful volumes are distilled from years of personal experience and research. In his approachable style, Paul Harris outlines his innovative strategy of 'simultaneous learning' as well as offering advice on lesson preparation, aural and memory work, effective practice and more.

0-571-52534-2   Improve your teaching!
0-571-53175-X   Improve your teaching! Teaching beginners
0-571-53319-1   Group Music Teaching in Practice (with ECD)

The Virtuoso Teacher

By considering *The Virtuoso Teacher* and how a teacher might attain virtuoso status, renowned educator and writer Paul Harris delves into the core issues of being a teacher and the teaching process. A fascinating look at topics such as self-awareness and the importance of emotional intelligence; getting the best out of pupils; dealing with challenging pupils; asking the right questions; creating a master-plan; taking the stress out of learning and teaching for the right reasons. This seminal book is an inspirational read for all music teachers, encouraging everyone to consider themselves in a new and uplifted light, and transform their teaching.

0-571-53676-X
The Virtuoso Teacher

The Simultaneous Learning Practice Map Pad

A revolutionary way to set up practice. Take a piece to be practised and write its title in the box; add words to describe the character of the piece underneath. Then set about filling in the significant features in the appropriate bubbles and begin working through these, drawing lines to make connections between them as you go along. You will achieve some really effective Simultaneous Practice!

0-571-59731-9
The Simultaneous Learning
Practice Map Pad

FABER *ff* MUSIC

Faber Music Ltd.
Burnt Mill
Elizabeth Way
Harlow
Essex
CM20 2HX

t   +44 (0)1279 828982
f   +44 (0)1279 828983
e   sales@fabermusic.com
w   www.fabermusicstore.com
     @fabermusic
     facebook.com/fabermusic

D minor

Fill in the scale: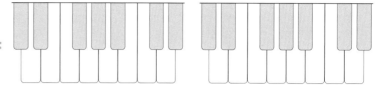

Write the key signature of D minor:

The relative major of D minor is: _____

TOP TIP Try practising your scales regularly with a metronome. See page 23 for a guide to tempo.

Finger fitness

Harmonic exercises

Arpeggio exercises

Melodic exercises

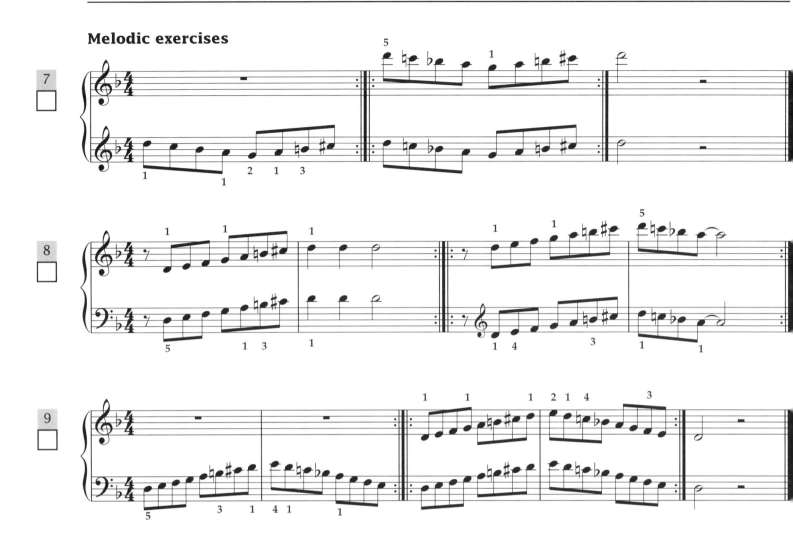

Key piece   **Doubloons**   Key piece using D harmonic minor

Key piece   Dance   Key piece using D melodic minor

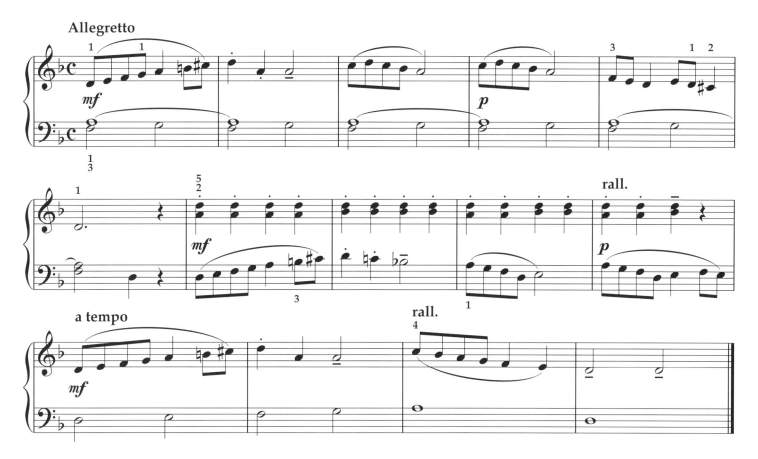

Have a go Using both hands, or just the right-hand line, compose or improvise an answering phrase or a short piece beginning with these notes:

Sight-reading

1 In which key is this piece?
2 Can you spot any repeated patterns?
3 Tap the pulse and try to hear the rhythm in your head.
4 Try to hear the music in your head before you begin.

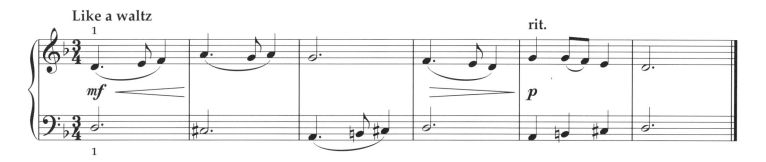

You are now ready to **say** the notes, **hear** the scale or broken chord in your head (playing the key note first), **think** about the fingering and then **play** the scale and arpeggio with confidence!

The complete scale and arpeggio are given on pages 24, 25 and 26.

G minor

Fill in the scale:

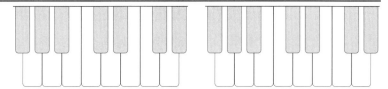

Write the key signature of G minor: _____

The relative major of G minor is: _____

Finger fitness

> **TOP TIP** G harmonic minor scale jumps from black key to black key, rather like a bridge.

1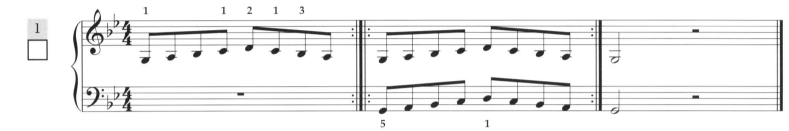

Harmonic exercises

2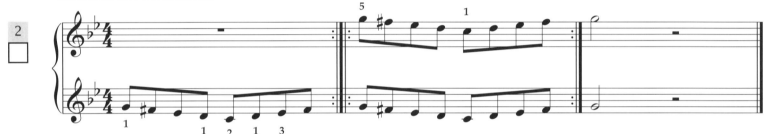

3

4

Arpeggio exercises

5

6

Melodic exercises

Key piece   Giza games   Key piece using G harmonic minor

2

Key piece   Graceful globefish   Key piece using G melodic minor

3

Have a go Using both hands, or just the right-hand line, compose or improvise an answering phrase or a short piece beginning with these notes:

4

Sight-reading

1 In which key is this piece?

2 Which notes are affected by the key signature? Explain the E natural and F sharp in bar 3, right hand.

3 Tap the rhythm of each line separately then both together.

4 Try to hear the music in your head before you begin.

5

You are now ready to **say** the notes, **hear** the scale or broken chord in your head (playing the key note first), **think** about the fingering and then **play** the scale and arpeggio with confidence!

Chromatic scale study

A chromatic (which literally means colourful) scale uses all the notes between any two key-notes. The most common fingering uses just 1, 2 and 3 (3 always plays a black note). Chromatic passages are usually showy, so should be played smoothly and fast, to impress!

• Make a 'C' shape with thumb and 3rd finger and start by playing all the notes from F to B♭ with the right and left hands. Make sure you keep the rest of the hand steady when you play.
• In the scale there are two places where there are two white notes together – the 2nd finger is used to fill in these white notes each time.
• Try a contrary chromatic scale starting on D to see how the fingering works symmetrically.
• Listen carefully for a smooth and unaccented musical line. To achieve an even legato, imagine falling gently from the black to the white notes.

Crispy chromatics   Chromatic study on D

Contrary motion scale studies

Contrary contraption   Contrary motion study in C major

Quite contrary   Contrary motion study in E major

Notice the black notes come together when playing this contrary motion scale.

Complete Grade 2 scales

For Grade 2 exams, the minimum tempo for scales is ♩ = 66. Try practising with a metronome, increasing the speed one notch at a time.

Exam requirements of the Associated Board:

- *G, D, A, F majors:* hands together and separately; 2 octaves
- *E, D, G minors:* hands together and separately; 2 octaves
- *Contrary motion scales:* C, E majors; hands beginning on the key-note (unison); 2 octaves
- *Chromatic scale beginning on D:* hands separately; 1 octave

G major

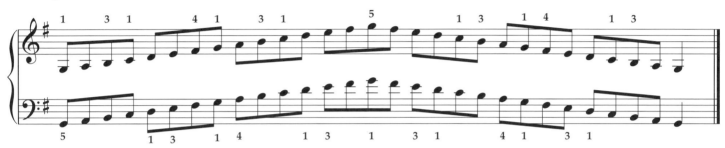

D major

A major

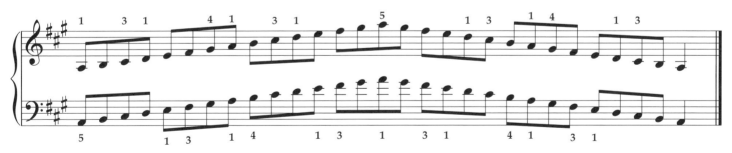

F major

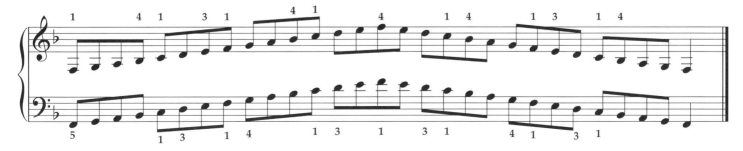

E minor harmonic

E minor melodic

D minor harmonic

D minor melodic

G minor harmonic

G minor melodic

C major contrary motion

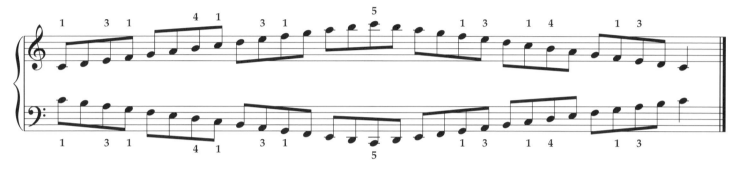

E major contrary motion

Right-hand chromatic scale

Left-hand chromatic scale

Complete Grade 2 arpeggios and broken chords

For Grade 2 exams, the minimum tempo is ♩ = 63. Try practising with a metronome, increasing the speed one notch at a time. Aim for a speed of about ♩ = 68.

Exam requirements of the Associated Board:

- *Arpeggios*: G, D, A majors and D, G minors: hands separately; 2 octaves
- *Broken chords*: F major, E minor: hands separately; according to pattern given below

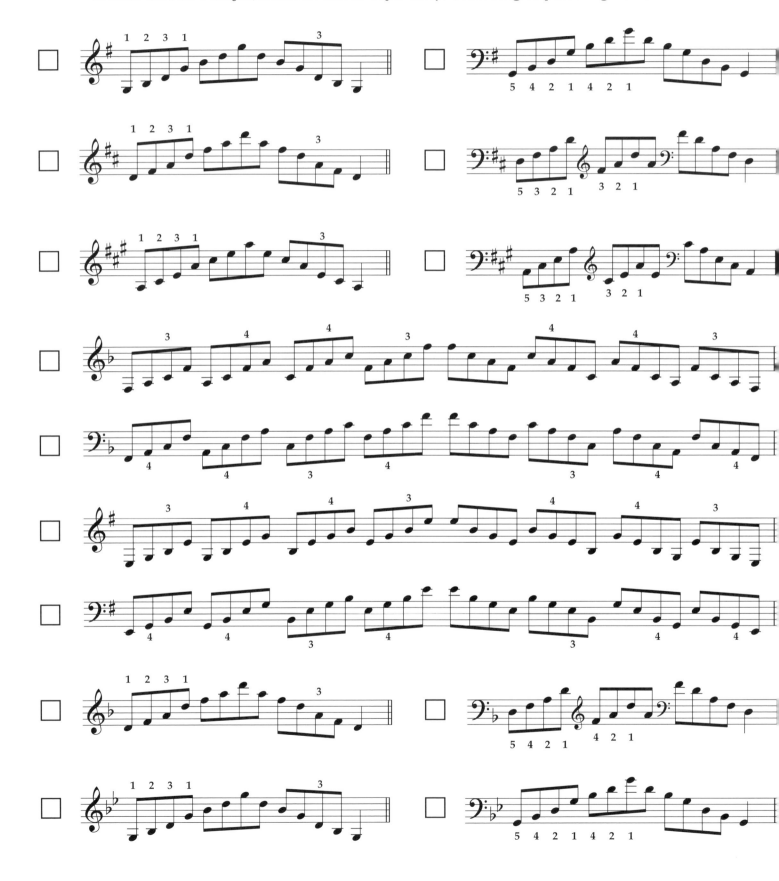

Why are scales important?

There are many reasons and it's important that pupils know them!

- Scales will hugely improve all aspects of your finger technique and control.
- Arpeggios will improve your ability to move around the piano with ease.
- Knowing your scales and arpeggios will speed up the learning of new pieces because so much material is usually based on scale and arpeggio patterns.
- Knowing your scales and arpeggios will improve your sight reading both in dealing with technical issues and reading melodic patterns.
- Knowing your scales and arpeggios will develop your sense of key.
- Playing scales and arpeggios well and with confidence will earn good marks in exams.

Scales and exams

So that's why scales are an important part of exams! They really do help to develop your playing. In an exam, the examiner will be listening out for:
- A prompt response
- Evenness of pulse and rhythm
- Control and evenness of tone
- No unnecessary accents
- The smooth passage of the thumb
- A sense of key
- Fluency and dexterity
- A musical shape for each example

Think about each of these during practice sessions. Tick them off in your mind.

© 2010 Faber Music Ltd
First published in 1995 by Faber Music Ltd
Bloomsbury House 74–77 Great Russell Street London WC1B 3DA
Music processed by Donald Thomson
Cover and text designed by Susan Clarke
Printed in England by Caligraving Ltd

ISBN10: 0-571-53412-0
EAN13: 978-0-571-53412-8

To buy Faber Music publications or to find out about the full range of titles
available please contact your local music retailer or Faber Music sales enquiries:
Faber Music Ltd, Burnt Mill, Elizabeth Way, Harlow CM20 2HX
Tel: +44 (0) 1279 82 89 82   Fax: +44 (0) 1279 82 89 83
sales@fabermusic.com   fabermusic.com

Practice chart

Practise your scales in different ways – with different rhythms
and dynamics and thinking of different colours and flavours!

Scale/Arpeggio	Comments	Tick a box each time you practise														
G major																
Scale																
Arpeggio																
D major																
Scale																
Arpeggio																
A major																
Scale																
Arpeggio																
F major																
Scale																
Broken chord																
E minor																
Scale																
Broken chord																
D minor																
Scale																
Arpeggio																
G minor																
Scale																
Arpeggio																
Contrary motion scale in C																
Contrary motion scale in E																
Chromatic scale on D (RH)																
Chromatic scale on D (LH)																